Knit One

Knit One

ANGELA KING

BOOK CLUB ASSOCIATES
LONDON

This edition published 1983 by
Book Club Associates
by arrangement with William Collins Sons & Co Ltd

© Knitting patterns Angela King 1983
© William Collins Sons & Co Ltd 1983

Reprinted 1984

Filmset in Souvenir by
Rowland Phototypesetting (London) Ltd
Printed in Italy by New Interlitho S.P.A.

This book is dedicated to the following knitters, without whose terrific and patient help the designs in the book would never have been knitted!

Debbie Ackerman	Dianne Howes
Barbara Barrington	Clare Hunt
Pat Brackenbury	Johanna King
Joan Cannell	Sally King
Penny Carnegie	Mary McDowell
Jean Dyott	Mrs Noble
Nora Giorgi	Miss Patrick (aged 92)
Linnie Goalen	Fusako Ridley
Mandy Goldman	Jane Stew
Connie Guzek	Mrs Thompson

The author and publishers gratefully acknowledge the help of the following magazines, wool companies and photographers who have given permission for their photographs to be reproduced in this book. Photographs were supplied courtesy of:

Cosmopolitan (Country Cousin – photograph: Toscani, Tender Touch – photograph: Tony McGee, Belle du Jour – photograph: Perry Ogden, Red Hot – photograph: Neil Kirk). Fashion editor and stylist: Caroline Baker.
Hayfield Textiles Ltd (Foxy Lady)
Living (School's Out)
The Observer Colour Magazine (Daisy)
Over 21 (Bel-Gazou)
She (Indian Summer – photograph: Peter Waldman)
Sunday supplement to The News of the World (Bowled Over – photograph: David Barnes)
H. G. Twilley Ltd (Colette, Claudine, Annie – photographs: Michael Murray)
Woman (Carved Ivory, Teddy Bear and Woolly Lamb, Ginger, Madame Butterfly, Geisha, Beginner's Luck, Coco, Lipstick, Shetland Lace, The French Lieutenant's Woman, Foxfire, Carrot Top)
Woman's Own (Snakeskin, Cassata, White Lady, New Yorker, High Society, Puffball)

FOR ADVICE ABOUT YARN

Pingouin,
(French Wools Ltd),
7-11 Lexington Street,
London, W1R 4BU
Tel: 01-439 8891

Patons and Baldwins Ltd,
Alloa, Clackmannanshire,
Scotland, FK10 1EG
Tel: Alloa (0259) 723431

Lister Lee Target,
PO Box 37,
Providence Mills, Wakefield,
West Yorkshire, WF2 9SF
Tel: Wakefield (0924) 75311

Sirdar Ltd,
PO Box 31,
Alverthorpe, Wakefield,
West Yorkshire
Tel: Wakefield (0924) 371501

H. G. Twilley Ltd,
Roman Mill, Stamford,
Lincolnshire, PE9 1BG
Tel: Stamford (0780) 52661

Hayfield Textiles Ltd,
Hayfield Mills,
Glusburn, Keighley,
West Yorkshire, BD20 8QP
Tel: Cross Hills (0535) 33333

Laines Couture,
20 Bedford Street,
London, WC2
Tel: 01-836 1805

A. N. I. (Art Needlework Industries) Ltd,
Ship Street,
Oxford, OX1 3DG
Tel: Oxford (0865) 47556

Laines Anny Blatt UK
48 Station Road,
Ossett, West Yorkshire
Tel: Ossett (0924) 262137

Contents

Introduction	9	New Yorker	55
Some Useful Advice	10	Sugar	56
Snakeskin	17	Coco	59
School's Out	18	Tender Touch	61
Carved Ivory	21	Belle du Jour	64
Foxy Lady	23	Lipstick	66
Country Cousin	27	Shetland Lace	68
Cassata	29	Red Hot	70
Colette	30	Daisy	73
Teddy Bear	32	The French Lieutenant's Woman	74
Woolly Lamb	34	Foxfire	77
Ginger	35	Claudine	78
Madame Butterfly	37	Annie	80
Double Take	40	High Society	83
Geisha	43	Carrot Top	85
Blazing Saddles	45	Bel-Gazou	87
Indian Summer	48	Bowled Over	88
Beginner's Luck	51	Puffball	90
White Lady	52	Tapestry	92

Introduction

If you love fashion, and you can knit, you have the most terrific advantage. A hand knitted sweater or jacket is an indispensable addition to any fashion wardrobe and beautiful, modern hand knitting patterns are now regularly featured in all the fashion magazines and in the national press. Hand knits are a practical investment, too. If you can't knit you have to buy them, and this is about ten times more expensive.

No longer is fashion concerned with one colour or length being 'out' or 'in'. The emphasis now is on expressing your individuality; on creating your own style and developing it. Fashion editors cover the trends, but also offer expert advice on how to work out what best suits you and your lifestyle. Self-expression is the most important thing and, with hand knitting, you can begin to express yourself on the first day you grasp how to knit and purl.

If you don't have much free time — and that must apply to almost everyone — it's the stylish, quick to knit patterns which make the most fashion sense. Simple classics are often the most effective to wear, anyway, and will give the longest fashion mileage. You'll feel a real sense of achievement after you've spent a lot of time working on a hand knitted masterpiece, but if you want something pretty to wear that you can rustle up in your odd free moments, stick to ultra-simple designs and concentrate on knitting them beautifully. A plain sweater in pristine cream wool or a cotton jacket in a bright colour is very quickly knitted, but looks stunning.

There are many easy and very easy patterns to knit in this book, as well as more complicated designs for knitters who love the mental and physical challenge of an intricate Fair Isle or a tricky lace stitch. This is quite a different sort of pleasure, but if you've never tackled a difficult pattern before, why not have a go? Take it slowly at first and you may be surprised at what you can achieve. You'll need patience more than anything else, and if you have plenty of that, no technique in knitting will be beyond your grasp.

Some Useful Advice

Many creative people are daunted by the technical side of knitting, which is a shame because learning the basics can be less painful than you think. If you had the time to read every knitting book ever printed, you would find that all the information they contain could be boiled down to the same fundamental points.

The best way to learn how to knit – and indeed how to do anything in knitting – is to get someone to show you. This is much the best method and will save you hours of puzzling over written instructions. Unfortunately the number of people who can demonstrate properly seems to be dwindling. Learning how to do things properly really is worth the effort, because it will make all the difference between an adequate result and something you can really be proud of. A knitting pattern is a *formula*, so study different patterns to see exactly what the formula is. Once you've cracked it, you will never have another problem.

The things you have to know

Tension
If you are following someone else's pattern, you *must* knit to tension. (Tension means how tightly or loosely your work is knitted.) However neat your knitting, if you haven't worked to tension – forget it! You are literally throwing away hours of work, as well as the cost of the wool. If you hate knitting a tension square, do a careful check on your actual work and measure the number of stitches and rows to the number of centimetres quoted at the top of the pattern. If you have fewer stitches than the given tension, change your needles to a size *smaller*. If you have more stitches than the given tension, change your needles to a size *larger*. Neglect to do this and you run the risk of your sweater turning into a perfectly knitted little straitjacket or string vest.

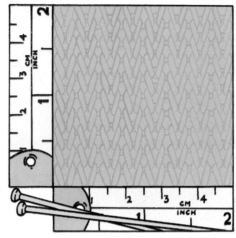

Tension

Abbreviations
If you are completely new to knitting you will never get *anywhere at all* unless you read the abbreviations. Abbreviations can be highly misleading: they are not standardised and one designer may use the same abbreviation as another but mean something completely different. So read the abbreviations at the beginning of the pattern; *never* assume you know what they mean.

Joining in yarn
If you don't want the sweater that you have spent hours knitting to come to pieces in your hands at some stage, it is better not to join in a new ball of yarn in the middle of a row; always join it in at the beginning of a row. (Any long ends will be useful for sewing up afterwards.)

Measurements
When I first started knitting, the section headed 'Measurements' was one I used to blithely ignore. Consequently, nothing ever turned out the right size. (It's the same story if you ignore tension!) If you want your garment to be the size the designer intended, you must check your measurements carefully. You must also check that the back has the same number of rows as the front to the armhole and to the shoulder and that each sleeve consists of exactly the same number of rows. The bad news is that you must therefore count every row of each piece of the garment. If you are checking stocking stitch, it is easier to count on the purl side.

Pressing
This is boring, but you'll be sorry if you don't! Not all knitting needs to be pressed: check the instructions on the ball band. If pressing is recommended and you don't bother, the garment will look badly rumpled – overdo it and you'll squash the stitches flat. (It's kill or cure, really.)

To press, pin out each piece to the correct measurement given in the pattern, with the wrong side of the work uppermost. Using a damp, dry or wet cloth (check the ball band again) and a warm iron, begin to press by raising and lowering the iron. *Never* move the iron back and forth as in ordinary ironing; once the iron has touched the cloth, it should only be raised straight up again. The pattern will tell you which parts of the garment need to be pressed.

Sewing up
It is possible to knit a garment beautifully, but if you sew it up badly you will fall at the last fence.

Invisible seaming An invisible seam is best for side seams and sleeve seams. You are going to sew two pieces together so you won't be able to see that there is a join. The trick is to sew with the *right side* of the pieces facing you. Place the two edges of each piece close together. Begin by securing the yarn at one end and bring the needle and yarn to the right side of the work. Bring the needle across and insert it under the thread that connects the first and second stitch of the row. Draw the needle and yarn through and then insert them through the same thread of the other piece of knitting. Continue to weave across the two pieces in this way, drawing them together firmly but not tightly.

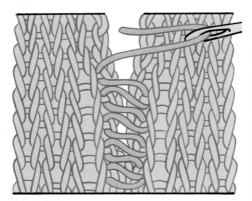

Invisible seaming

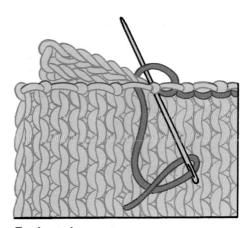

Back stitch seaming

Back stitch seaming Use a back stitch seam when the seam runs *across* the grain of the knitting, as in the shoulder seam or along a shaped edge. Place the two edges together with the right sides inside, and fasten the yarn at the right hand edge at the back of the work. Work the seam from right to left, moving one stitch to the right, at the front and two to the left at the back of the work.

How to knit

Casting on

I always cast on using the thumb method, but there are other methods as well.

Thumb method (using only one needle) Leaving a piece of yarn hanging down which is long enough to form the number of stitches required, make a slip loop and put it onto the needle. Hold the loose end of yarn in the left hand and make a loop on the left thumb (a). Insert the needle into this loop (b), wrap the yarn round the needle (c) and draw it through the loop on the thumb (d) as you slip the loop from the thumb and gently tighten the left hand thread (e). You have now formed the first stitch. Repeat the process for the rest of the row.

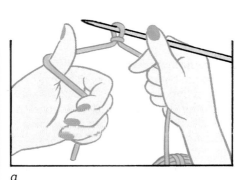

a

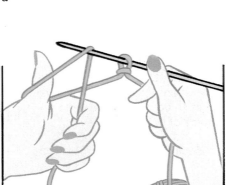

b

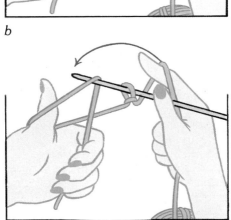

c

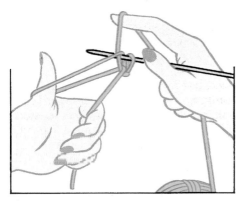

d

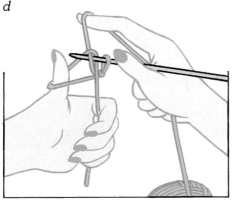

e

The two needle method Make a slip loop and place it on the left hand needle. Insert the right hand needle into it, wind the yarn round the right hand needle, draw a loop through and place this loop onto the left hand needle. Continue in this way, working into the last stitch on the left hand needle each time.

Casting off

Knit the first two stitches of the row. With the point of the left hand needle, lift the stitch furthest to the right on the right hand needle over the stitch next to it, leaving one stitch on the right hand needle. Knit one more stitch, making two stitches on the right hand needle. Lift the one furthest to the right over the other, as before. Continue in this way until only one stitch of the row remains. Cut the yarn and pass it through this stitch to fasten off.

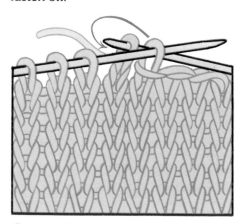

Casting off

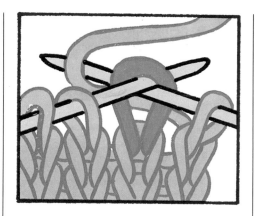

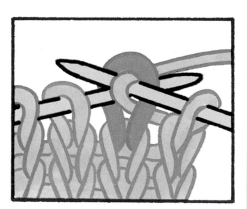

How to knit a stitch

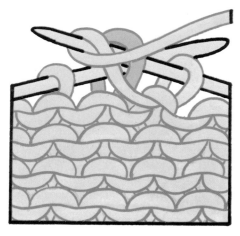

How to purl a stitch

Knitting and purling

How to knit a stitch Hold the needle with the cast on stitches in the left hand. With the yarn at the back of the work, insert the right hand needle into the front of the first loop on the left hand needle, front to back, left to right. Wind the yarn round the point of the right hand needle and draw a loop through the loop on the left hand needle, while slipping this left hand stitch. The new stitch is now on the right hand needle. Continue in this way until there are no more stitches on the left hand needle. Transfer the right hand needle to the left hand and begin the second row.

How to purl a stitch Hold the needle with the cast on stitches in the left hand. With the yarn at the front of the work, insert the right hand needle into the front of the first stitch, back to front, right to left. Take the yarn round the point of the right hand needle over the top and under, from right to left. Draw this loop through the stitch on the left hand needle, while slipping the left hand stitch. The new stitch is now on the right hand needle. Continue in this way until there are no more stitches on the left hand needle, then start a new row.

Some simple stitches

Garter stitch
This means that you knit *every* stitch of every row.

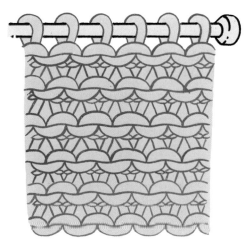

Garter stitch

Stocking stitch
You knit the first row and purl the second row, repeating these two rows throughout.

Stocking stitch

Reversed stocking stitch
Work this in the same way as stocking stitch, but the *purl* side is the right side of the work.

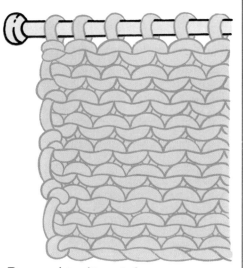

Reversed stocking stitch

Moss stitch
You knit the first stitch and purl the next stitch, continuing in this way to the end of the row. On the second row, you work the opposite of the stitch as it faces you (in other words, you purl the knit stitches that face you, and knit the purl stitches that face you).

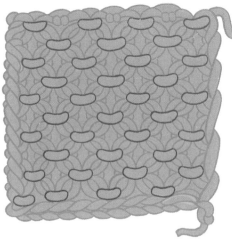

Moss stitch

The dirty tricks department

You should not do any of the following things unless you have *absolutely no alternative.*

Switching yarns
It is always best to use the yarn recommended in the 'Materials' section of the pattern. However, if you love the design but the recommended yarn is too expensive, or if the pattern uses a yarn such as cotton that you are unwilling to try, it is possible to knit the garment in another yarn. If you do this, however, you *must* knit a tension square and achieve the right tension with the new yarn before you make the switch. The new yarn obviously must be of a comparable thickness.

Mixing yarns
Wool companies are very much against knitters using many different types of yarn together. However, this is an excellent way of using up all those odd balls of yarn, but once again remember that the ones you do use must all be of a comparable thickness, otherwise you'll have a tension problem. If some of the yarns are much thinner, you can get round this by using them double, or even treble. Mixing yarns is a marvellous way to experiment if you love to create original textures and effects, and it's highly economical if you have a lot of leftover yarn.

Pulling threads
To operate this one – and it's not for the fainthearted – you need a lot of confidence and the certainty that you know what you are doing. If you own a much-loved sweater and the ribbing has worn out, or it has stretched in the wash and is

far too long, or too much wearing has made a garment baggy round the bottom, it is possible to pull a thread to enable you to reknit the ribbing only, or to shorten the garment by unravelling some rows and then reknitting the ribbing.

With a sharp pair of scissors, very, very carefully cut the head of *one* stitch near the end of the row just above the ribbing (having previously undone the side seams). Now gently separate the rib from the main part, picking up the stitches at the base of the main part as you go. It is now possible to knit the rib *downwards*, remembering to cast off firmly.

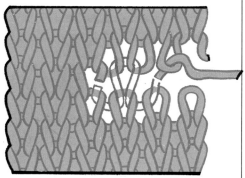

Pulling threads

Swiss darning over Fair Isle mistakes
If you have knitted a complicated Fair Isle and your eagle eye has spotted *one* minute mistake, obviously you will pull the whole thing undone and reknit it from scratch. However, if you simply don't have any more time, Swiss darn in the correct colour over the incorrect stitch, by threading a darning needle with the correct shade of yarn and working it over the mistake as shown in the diagram.

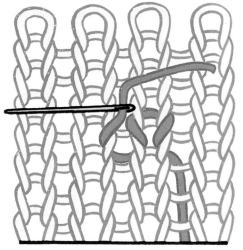

Swiss darning

Bribing someone to knit it for you
If you love expensive looking hand knits but loathe knitting, don't soldier on, hating every second. Trade services with a friend who loves to knit, or ingratiate yourself with your granny. If all else fails, you can always type out an advertisement for an experienced knitter and display it at your local newsagents: I've found loads of good knitters that way.

Patterns

Snakeskin

MATERIALS

11 (12, 13, 14) 20 g. balls Sirdar Wash 'n' Wear 4-ply; a pair each 3¼ mm. (no. 10) and 3¾ mm. (no. 9) knitting needles; a 3¼ mm. (no. 10) Aero circular twin-pin, 90 cm. long; 15 (16, 18, 19) strings of 1,000 8 mm. knitting sequins.

TENSION

26 stitches and 34 rows to 10 cm. square.

MEASUREMENTS

To fit bust 32 (34, 36, 38) in., 81 (86, 91, 97) cm. closely (actual size 33½ (36, 38, 39¾) in., 85 (91, 96, 101) cm. including wrap-over.)
Length 20¾ (21¾, 22½, 23) in , 53 (55, 57, 59) cm.
Sleeve seam (all sizes) 17 in., 43 cm.

ABBREVIATIONS

k., knit; p., purl; st(s)., stitch(es); alt., alternate; beg., beginning; cont., continue; dec., decreas(e)(ing); foll., following; inc., increas(e)(ing); k.b., knit into back of stitch; patt., pattern; p.s.s.o., pass slip stitch over; rem., remaining; rep., repeat; s.1, sequin one thus: push a sequin up close to back of work, k. next st. then push sequin through st. to front; sl., slip; st. st., stocking stitch; t.b.l., through back of loop; tog., together.

INSTRUCTIONS

Back

Thread equal number of sequins on to each ball, leaving one free. This ball is to be used for hems and facing. With 3¼ mm. needles, cast on 109 (115, 121, 127) sts. Beg. k. row, work 7 rows in st. st. (see page 13).
Next row (hemline): K. into the back of each st. Change to 3¾ mm. needles and

patt. thus:
Row 1: K.b.1, (s.1, k.b.1) to end.
Row 2: P.
Row 3: (K.b.1) twice, (s.1, k.b.1) to last st., k.b.1.
Row 4: P.
These rows form the patt. *. Cont. in patt. until work measures 32 (33, 34, 35) cm. from hemline, ending with a p. row.

To shape armholes Cast off 4 sts. at beg. of next 4 rows. Dec. 1 st. at both ends of next row and foll. alt. rows until 81 (87, 93, 99) sts. remain. Cont. straight until armholes measure 21 (22, 23, 24) cm., ending with a p. row.

To shape shoulders Cast off 7 (8, 8, 9) sts. at beg. of next 4 rows and 7 (7, 9, 9) sts. at beg. of next 2 rows. Cast off rem. sts.

Left front

With 3¼ mm. needles, cast on 59 (63, 67, 71) sts. Work as Back to *. Cont. in patt. until work measures 29 (30, 30, 31) cm. from hemline, ending with a p. row.

To shape front Dec. 1 st. at end of next row and at same edge on every foll. third row until work matches Back to armhole, ending with a p. row.

To shape armhole Still dec. at neck edge as before, cast off 4 sts. at beg. of next row and foll. alt. row; then dec. 1 st. at armhole edge on foll. 6 alt. rows. Keeping armhole edge straight, cont. dec. at neck edge until 21 (23, 25, 27) sts. remain. Cont. straight until Front matches Back to shoulder, ending side edge.

To shape shoulder Cast off 7 (8, 8, 9) sts. at beg. of next row and foll. alt. row. Work 1 row. Cast off rem. 7 (7, 9, 9) sts.

Right front

Work as Left Front, reversing shapings.

Sleeves

With 3¼ mm. needles, cast on 53 (57, 61, 65) sts. Work as Back to *. Cont. in patt. inc. 1 st. at both ends of twenty-ninth row and every foll. sixth row until there are 85 (89, 93, 97) sts. Cont. straight until sleeve measures 43 cm. from hemline, ending with a p. row.

To shape top Cast off 4 sts. at beg. of next 2 rows; dec. 1 st. at both ends of next row and foll. alt. rows until 33 sts. remain, ending with a p. row. Cast off 3 sts. at beg. of next 4 rows. Cast off rem. sts.

Facing

Join shoulder seams. With 3¼ mm. circular needle and right side facing beg. at hemline, pick up and k. 80 (84, 84, 88) sts. up right front to neck shaping, 1 st. from corner (mark this st.), 62 (66, 70, 74) sts. up shaped edge of right front to shoulder, 39 (41, 43, 45) sts. from back neck, 62 (66, 70, 74) sts. down shaped edge of front, 1 st. from corner (mark this st.), 80 (84, 84, 88) sts. down left front to hemline – 325 (343, 353, 371) sts. Working backwards and forwards on these sts., k. 1 row.
Next row: K. to 2 sts. before marked st., k. 2 tog., k. 1, sl. 1, k. 1, p.s.s.o., (k. to shoulder, inc. in each of next 2 sts.) twice, k. to 2 sts. before next marked st., k. 2 tog., k. 1, sl. 1, k. 1, p.s.s.o., k. to end.
Next row: P.
Rep. last 2 rows twice more. Cast off.

TO MAKE UP

Do not press. Join side and sleeve seams. Sew in sleeves. Turn hems and facing to wrong side and slip-stitch.

School's Out

MATERIALS

7 (8) 50 g. balls Hayfield Brig D.K.; a pair each 3¼ mm. (no. 10) and 4 mm. (no. 8) knitting needles; a cable needle; a 3¼ mm. (no. 10) circular knitting needle, 60 cm. long; a stitch-holder.

TENSION

18 stitches and 20 rows to 7 cm. over pattern between cables.

MEASUREMENTS

To fit bust 32-34 (36-38) in., 81-87 (91-97) cm.
Back length 22½ (23¼) in., 57 (59) cm.

ABBREVIATIONS

k., knit; p., purl; st(s)., stitch(es); alt., alternate; beg., beginning; cont., continue; C10B, cable 10 back by slipping the next 5 sts. onto a cable needle and holding at the back of work, k. 5, then k. 5 from cable needle; C10F, cable 10 forward by slipping the next 5 sts. onto cable needle and holding at the front of work, k. 5, then k. 5 from cable needle; dec., decreas(e)(ing); inc., increas(e)(ing); patt., pattern; rem., remaining; rep., repeat; RS, right side; tog., together; WS, wrong side.

INSTRUCTIONS

Back

With 3¼ mm. needles, cast on 122 (134) sts. Work 5 cm. in k. 2, p. 2 rib, beg. WS rows, p. 2, and *inc. 1 st. at each end of last row for 2nd size only* – 122 (136) sts.
Change to 4 mm. needles and work as follows:
Row 1 (RS): (P. 2, k. 5) three (four) times, p. 2, k. 10, * (p. 2, k. 5) three times, p. 2, k. 10, rep. from * once, (p. 2, k. 5) three (four) times, p. 2.
Row 2: (K. 2, p. 5) three (four) times, k. 2, p. 10, * (k. 2, p. 5) three times, k. 2,

---

Classic Aran slipover with a preppie look.
Easy

---

p. 10, rep. from * once, (k. 2, p. 5) three (four) times, k. 2.
Row 3: P. 23 (30), k. 10, (p. 23, k. 10) twice, p. 23 (30).
Rows 4, 6, 8, 10, 12, 14 and 16: As row 2.
Row 5 and 13: As row 1.
Rows 7, 11 and 15: As row 3.
Row 9: (P. 2, k. 5) three (four) times, p. 2, C10F, (p. 2, k. 5) three times, p. 2, C10B, (p. 2, k. 5) three times, p. 2, C10F, (p. 2, k. 5) three (four) times, p. 2.
These 16 rows form patt. Cont. in patt. until work measures 36 (37) cm. from cast-on edge, ending with a WS row.

To shape armhole Keeping patt. correct, cast off 4 sts. at beg. of next 2 rows. Dec. 1 st. at each end of the next 3 RS rows – 108 (122) sts. **.
Cont. straight until work measures 17 (18) cm. from beg. of armhole shaping, ending with a WS row.

To shape neck Next row: Patt. 36 (41), turn; cont. on these sts. only for first side, leaving rem. sts. on a spare needle. Dec. 1 st. at neck edge on every row until 26 (29) sts. remain. Cast off.
With RS facing, slip centre 36 (40) sts. onto a stitch-holder. Rejoin yarn and complete other side of neck to match, reversing shaping.

Front

Work as Back to **. Cont. straight until work measures 7 (8) cm. from beg. of armhole shaping, ending with a WS row.

To shape neck Next row: Patt. 52 (59), k. 2 tog.; cont. on these sts. only, leaving rem. sts. on a spare needle. Dec. 1 st. at neck edge on the next 18 (26) rows, then on every alt. row until 26 (29) sts. remain. Cont. straight until work measures same as Back to shoulder, then cast off.

With RS facing, rejoin yarn to inner end of rem. 54 (61) sts. K. 2 tog., patt. to end. Complete to match first side.

Neckband

Join shoulders. With RS facing and circular 3¼ mm. needle, pick up and k. 10 (14) sts. down right back neck, k. across the 36 (40) sts. on stitch-holder, pick up and k. 10 (14) sts. up left back neck, 42 sts. down left front neck, 2 sts. from centre and 42 sts. up right front neck – 142 (154) sts. Work 8 rounds in k. 2, p. 2 rib, but dec. 1 st. at either side of the 2 sts. at centre front on every round. Cast off ribwise, dec. as before.

Armbands

With RS facing and 3¼ mm. needles, pick up and k. 114 (122) sts. evenly along armhole. Work 8 rows in k. 2, p. 2 rib, beg. alt. rows p. 2, then cast off ribwise.

TO MAKE UP

Join side seams and armband seams. Press all seams.

Carved Ivory

Delicately patterned Aran sweater with slightly square shoulders, which uses the finer Aran stitches.

MATERIALS

13 (14, 15) 50 g. balls Hayfield Brig D.K.; a pair each 3¼ mm. (no. 10) and 3¾ mm. (no. 9) knitting needles; two cable needles; a stitch-holder; two shoulder pads (optional).

TENSION

17 stitches to 5 cm. (slightly stretched) and 24 rows to 7 cm.

MEASUREMENTS

To fit bust 34 (36, 38) in., 86 (91, 97) cm.
Length 21¼ (21¾, 22) in., 54 (55, 56) cm.
Sleeve (all sizes) 17 in., 43 cm.

ABBREVIATIONS

k., knit; p., purl; st(s)., stitch(es); beg., beginning; cont., continue; c. 6 b., cable 6 back; c. 6 f., cable 6 forward; c. 4 l., cable 4 left; c. 4 r., cable 4 right; cr. 6, cross 6; cr. 2 r., cross 2 right; cr. 2 l., cross 2 left; c. 3 r., cable 3 right; c. 3 l., cable 3 left; dec., decrease; foll., following; inc., increase; m. 1, make one; patt., pattern; rep., repeat; sl., slip; t. 2 l., twist 2 left; t. 2 r., twist 2 right; t. 2 r. p., twist 2 right purl; t. 2 l. p., twist 2 left purl; tog., together; t.b.l., through back of loop.

INSTRUCTIONS

Back
With 3¼ mm. needles, cast on 126 (134, 142) sts. Work 15 rows in k. 2, p. 2 rib, beg. second row p. 2.
Inc. row: Rib 5 (5, 8), * inc. in next st., rib 4, inc. in next st., rib 4 (3, 2); rep. from * eleven (thirteen, fifteen) times, rib 1 (3, 6) – 150 (162, 174) sts.
Change to 3¾ mm. needles and patt. thus:
Row 1 (right side): P. 4, * k. 4, p. 2, sl. next st. onto cable needle and leave at back, k. next st., p. st. from cable needle (referred to as cr. 2 r.), sl. next st. onto cable needle and leave at front, p. next st., k. st. from cable needle (referred to as cr. 2 l.), p. 2 (k. 4, p. 2) two (three, four) times, cr. 2 r., cr. 2 l., p. 2, k. 4 *, p. 4, ** sl. next st. onto cable needle and leave at front, k. next st., k. st. from cable needle (referred to as t. 2 l.), p. 2, k. 4, p. 2, t. 2 l., p. 2 **; rep. from ** to ** once, (p. 2, k. 2) twice, p. 4; rep. from ** to ** twice, p. 2; rep. from * to * once, p. 4.
Row 2: K. 4, * p. 4, k. 2, (p. 1, k. 2) twice, (p. 4, k. 2) two (three, four) times, (p. 1, k. 2) twice, p. 4 *, k. 4, ** p. 2, k. 2, p. 4, k. 2, p. 2, k. 2 **; rep. from ** to ** once, (k. 2, p. 2) twice, k. 4; rep. from ** to ** twice, k. 2; rep. from * to * once, k. 4.
Row 3: P. 4, * sl. next 2 sts. onto cable needle and leave at back, k. next 2 sts., k. 2 sts. from cable needle (referred to as c. 4 r.), p. 2, cr. 2 l., cr. 2 r., p. 2, (c. 4 r., p. 2) two (three, four) times, cr. 2 l., cr. 2 r., p. 2, c. 4 r. *, p. 4, ** t. 2 l., p. 2, sl. next 2 sts. onto cable needle and leave at front, k. 2, k. 2 sts. from cable needle (referred to as c. 4 l.), p. 2, t. 2 l., p. 2 **; rep. from ** to ** once, p. 2, sl. next 2 sts. onto cable needle and leave at back, sl. next 2 sts. onto second cable needle and leave at front, k. next 2 sts., p. 2 sts. from front cable needle, k. 2 sts. from back cable needle (referred to as cr. 6), p. 4; rep. from ** to ** twice, p. 2; rep. from * to * once, p. 4.
Row 4: K. 4, * p. 4, k. 3, p. 2, k. 3, (p. 4, k. 2) two (three, four) times, k. 1, p. 2, k. 3, p. 4 *, k. 4, ** p. 2, k. 2, p. 4, k. 2, p. 2, k. 2 **; rep. from ** to ** once, (k. 2, p. 2) twice, k. 4; rep. from ** to ** twice, k. 2; rep. from * to * once, k. 4.
These 4 rows form patt. for side panels now referred to as patt. 38 (44, 50).
Row 5: As row 1.
Row 6: As row 2.
Row 7: Patt. 38 (44, 50), p. 4; rep. from ** to ** of row 1 twice, (p. 2, k. 2) twice, p. 4; rep. from ** to ** of row 1 twice, p. 2, patt. 38 (44, 50).
Row 8: As row 4.
Row 9: Patt. 38 (44, 50), p. 4; rep. from ** to ** of row 3 twice, (p. 2, k. 2) twice, p. 4; rep. from ** to ** of row 3 twice, p. 2, patt. 38 (44, 50).
Row 10: As row 2.
Row 11: As row 7.
Row 12: As row 4.
These 12 rows form patt. Work patt. until work measures 35 cm. from beg.

To shape armhole Cast off 7 (9, 9) sts. at beg. of next 2 rows and 4 (5, 6) sts. at beg. of foll. 2 rows. Dec. 1 st. at beg. of next 8 (10, 12) rows – 120 (124, 132) sts.
*** Cont. straight until work measures 50 (51, 52) cm. from beg., ending with a wrong side row.

To shape neck *Next row:* Patt. 43 (45, 48), turn. Cont. on these sts. only. Dec. 1 st. at neck edge on next 8 rows. Patt. 5 rows. Cast off. Sl. centre 34 (34, 36) sts. onto a stitch-holder, rejoin yarn and work other side to match.

Front
As Back to ***. Cont. straight until work measures 45 (46, 47) cm., ending with a wrong side row.

To shape neck *Next row:* Patt. 46 (48, 51), turn. Cont. on these sts. only. Dec. 1 st. at neck edge on next 11 rows. Work 18 rows straight. Cast off. Sl. centre 28 (28, 30) sts. onto a stitch-holder, rejoin yarn and work other side to match.

Sleeves
With 3¼ mm. needles, cast on 70 sts. Rib 15 rows as Back.
Inc. row: Rib 4, * inc. in next st., rib 3; rep. from * fifteen times, rib 2 – 86 sts.
Patt. thus:
Row 1 (right side): P. 4, * k. 4, p. 2, cr. 2 r., cr. 2 l., p. 2, k. 4 *, p. 4; rep. from ** to ** of row 1 of Back once, (p. 2, k. 2) twice, p. 4; rep. from ** to ** of row 1 of Back once, p. 2; rep. from * to * once, p. 4.

Row 2: K. 4, * p. 4, k. 2, (p. 1, k. 2) twice, p. 4 *, k. 4; rep. from ** to ** of row 2 of Back once, (k. 2, p. 2) twice, k. 4; rep. from ** to ** of row 2 of Back once, k. 2; rep. from * to * once, k. 4.

Row 3: P. 4, * c. 4 r., p. 2, cr. 2 l., cr. 2 r., p. 2, c. 4 r. *, p. 4; rep. from ** to ** of row 3 of Back once, p. 2, cr. 6, p. 4; rep. from ** to ** of row 3 of Back once, p. 2; rep. from * to * once, p. 4. Cont. in patt. as set, inc. 1 st. at each end of second and every foll. sixth row (working these inc. sts. in t. 2 l., p. 2 rib) until there are 112 (122, 128) sts. Cont. straight until work measures 43 cm.

To shape top Cast off 7 (9, 9) sts. at beg. of next 2 rows and 4 (5, 6) sts. at beg. of foll. 2 rows. Dec. 1 st. at beg. of every row until 48 sts. remain. Cast off 6 sts. at beg. of next 4 rows. Cast off.

Neckband

Join right shoulder seam. With 3¼ mm. needles and right side facing, pick up and k. 29 (29, 28) sts. down left side of front, across centre front sts. k. 1 (1, 2), p. 2, (k. 2, p. 2) six times, k. 1 (1, 2), pick up and k. 29 (29, 28) sts. up right side of neck, 12 (12, 11) sts. down right side of back, k. 0 (0, 1), p. 2, (k. 2, p. 2) eight times, k. 0 (0, 1), pick up and k. 12 (12, 11) sts. up left side of back – 144 (144, 144) sts. Beg. k. 2, work 7 rows in k. 2, p. 2 rib. Cast off ribwise.

TO MAKE UP

Do not press. Join right shoulder and neckband seam. Set in sleeves. Join side and sleeve seams. Press seams lightly. Fit shoulder pads if required.

Foxy Lady

MATERIALS

17 (19) 50 g. balls Hayfield Grampian D.K. (shade 33015 – cream) or 25 (27) 50 g. balls Hayfield Brig D.K.; a pair each 4 mm. (no. 8), 3¾ mm. (no. 9) and 3¼ mm. (no. 10) knitting needles; one spare double pointed needle; two shoulder pads.

TENSION

16 stitches to 5 cm. using 4 mm. needles; and 12 stitches to 5 cm. using 3¾ mm. needles.

MEASUREMENTS

To fit bust 34-36 (38-40) in., 86-91 (97-102) cm. (actual size 42½ (45½) in., 108 (116) cm.)
Approx. length 38½ (39) in., 98 (99) cm.
Sleeve (both sizes) 17½ in., 44 cm.

ABBREVIATIONS

k., knit; p., purl; st(s)., stitch(es); beg., beginning; cont., continue; dec., decrease; foll., following; inc., increase; k. 1B., knit into back of stitch; patt., pattern; rem., remaining; rep., repeat; sl., slip; tog., together; y. fd., yarn forward.

NOTES

After casting off stitches for shaping, one stitch will remain on the right hand needle which is not included in the instructions that follow.
Remember to check your tension over each different band of stitches.

> **Unusual treatment of Aran: the stitches form horizontal bands instead of travelling vertically. Cables, trellis stitch and bobble stitch make up the pattern and, providing you check your tension carefully for each pattern, you can't go wrong.**

INSTRUCTIONS

Back
With 3¼ mm. needles, cast on 149 (157) sts.
Row 1: Sl. 1, k. 1, * p. 1, k. 1; rep. from * to last st., k. 1.
Row 2: Sl. 1, * p. 1, k. 1; rep. from * to end.
Rep. rows 1 and 2 twice, then row 1 once more.
1st size only: Row 8: Sl. 1, p. 1, k. 1, p. 1, * inc. into next st., (p. 1, k. 1) three times, inc. into next st. purlwise, (k. 1, p. 1) three times; rep. from * to last 5 sts., inc. once into next st., (p. 1, k. 1) twice – 170 sts.
2nd size only: Row 8: Inc. into first st., p. 1, (k. 1, p. 1) twice, * inc. into next st., (p. 1, k. 1) three times, inc. into next st. purlwise, k. 1, (p. 1, k. 1) twice, inc. into next st. purlwise, (k. 1, p. 1) three times, inc. into next st., p. 1, (k. 1, p. 1) twice; rep. from * to last 21 sts., inc. into next st., (p. 1, k. 1) three times, inc. into next st. purlwise, k. 1, (p. 1, k. 1) twice, inc. into next st. purlwise) twice, k. 1 – 182 sts.
For both sizes: ** Change to 4 mm. needles and work Trellis patt. as follows:
Row 1: Sl. 1, k. 1, * p. 4, k. 2; rep. from * to end.
Row 2: Sl. 1, p. 1, * k. 4, p. 2; rep. from * to last 6 sts., k. 4, p. 1, k. 1.
Row 3: As row 1.
Row 4: As row 2.
Row 5: Sl. 1, * (sl. next st. onto spare needle and hold at front of work, p. 2, then k. st. from spare needle – called C3F), (slip next 2 sts. onto spare needle and hold at back of work, k. 1, then purl 2 sts. from spare needle – called C3B); rep. from * to last st., k. 1.
Row 6: Sl. 1, k. 2, * p. 2, k. 4; rep. from *

to last 5 sts., p. 2, k. 3.
Row 7: Sl. 1, p. 2, k. 2, * p. 4, k. 2; rep. from * to last 3 sts., p. 2, k. 1.
Row 8: As row 6.
Row 9: As row 7.
Row 10: As row 6.
Row 11: Sl. 1, * C3B, C3F; rep. from * to last st., k. 1.
Row 12: Sl. 1, p. 1, * k. 4, p. 2; rep. from * to last 6 sts., k. 4, p. 1, k. 1.
These 12 rows form Trellis patt.
Cont. in Trellis patt. until this patt. measures 11 cm., ending with a wrong side row.
Now work Cable patt. thus:
Row 1: Sl. 1, p. 3, * k. 6, p. 6; rep. from * to last 10 sts., k. 6, p. 3, k. 1.
Row 2: Sl. 1, k. 3, p. 6, * k. 6, p. 6; rep. from * to last 4 sts., k. 4.
Row 3: As row 1.
Row 4: As row 2.
Row 5: Sl. 1, p. 3, * (sl. next 3 sts. onto spare needle and hold at back of work, k. 3, then k. 3 sts. from spare needle called C6B), p. 6; rep. from * to last 10 sts., C6B, p. 3, k. 1.
Row 6: As row 2.
Rep. rows 1 and 2 twice more, then row 1 once more.
Row 12: Sl. 1, k. 3, p. 6, * k. 6, p. 6; rep. from * to last 4 sts., k. 4.
These 12 rows form Cable patt. Cont. in Cable patt. until this patt. measures 11 cm., ending with a wrong side row.
1st size only: Next row: Sl. 1, k. 2 tog., k. 1, * k. 2 tog., k. 2; rep. from * to last 6 sts., (k. 2 tog., k. 1) twice – 127 sts.
2nd size only: Next row: Sl. 1, k. 5, k. 2 tog., * k. 2, k. 2 tog.; rep. from * to last 6 sts., k. 6 – 139 sts.
For both sizes: Next row: Sl. 1, p. to last st., k. 1.
Change to 3¾ mm. needles and work Bobble patt. thus:
Row 1: Sl. 1, k. 2, * (k. 1, y. fd., k. 1, y. fd., k. 1, k. 1B, all into next st., sl. second, third, fourth, fifth and sixth sts. over first st. – called MB), k. 5; rep. from * to last 4 sts., MB, k. 3.
Row 2: Sl. 1, p. to last st., k. 1.
Row 3: Sl. 1, k. to end.
Row 4: Sl. 1, p. to last st., k. 1.
Row 5: Sl. 1, k. 5, * MB, k. 5; rep. from * to last 7 sts., MB, k. 6.
Row 6: Sl. 1, p. to last st., k. 1.

Row 7: Sl. 1, k. to end.
Row 8: Sl. 1, p. to last st., k. 1.
These 8 rows form Bobble patt. Cont. in Bobble patt. until this patt. measures 11 cm., ending with a right side row.
1st size only: Next row: Inc. into first st., p. 1, * inc. into next st. purlwise, p. 2; rep. from * to last 2 sts., inc. into next st. purlwise, k. 1 – 170 sts. **.
2nd size only: Next row: Sl. 1, p. 5, * inc. into next st. purlwise, p. 2; rep. from * to last 7 sts., inc. into next st. purlwise, p. 5, k. 1 – 182 sts. **.
For both sizes: Rep. from ** to ** once. Change to 4 mm. needles and cont. in Trellis patt. until this patt. measures 4 cm., ending with a wrong side row.

To shape armholes Cast off 8 sts. in patt. at beg. of next 2 rows, then 6 sts. at beg. of foll. 2 rows. Work 10 rows but dec. 1 st. at each end of every row – 122 (134) sts.
Cont. without shaping until Trellis patt. measures 11 cm., ending with a wrong side row ***. Now work Cable patt. until this patt. measures 11 cm., ending with a wrong side row.
1st size only: Next row: Sl. 1, k. 2 tog., k. 1, * k. 2 tog., k. 2; rep. from * to last 6 sts., (k. 2 tog., k. 1) twice – 91 sts.
2nd size only: Next row: Sl. 1, k. 5, k. 2 tog., * k. 2, k. 2 tog.; rep. from * to last 6 sts., k. 6 – 103 sts.
For both sizes: Next row: Sl. 1, p. to last st., k. 1.
Change to 3¾ mm. needles and in Bobble patt. work as follows:
Work 6 rows.

To shape neck *Next row:* Sl. 1, patt. 30 (34), cast off 29 (33) sts., patt. to last st., k. 1.
Working on first 31 (35) sts. only, work as follows:
Next row: Sl. 1, patt. to last st., k. 1. Work 8 (10) rows, but dec. 1 st. at neck edge on every row – 23 (25) sts. (Length of armhole should measure approx. 23 (24) cm.) Cast off in patt.
With wrong side facing, rejoin yarn to rem. 31 (35) sts. and work as follows:
Next row: K. 1, patt. to last st., k. 1. Work 8 (10) rows, but dec. 1 st. at neck edge on every row – 23 (25) sts. Cast off in patt.

Front

Exactly as Back to ***.
Cont. in Cable patt. until it is 8 rows less than previous Cable patt.

To shape neck *Next row:* Sl. 1, patt. 45 (49), cast off 30 (34) sts., patt. to last st., k. 1.
Working on first 46 (50) sts. only, work as follows:
Next row: Sl. 1, patt. to last st., k. 1.
Work 6 rows in patt., but dec. 1 st. at neck edge on every row – 40 (44) sts.
1st size only: Next row: * K. 2, k. 2 tog.; rep. from * to last 4 sts., k. 1, k. 2 tog., k. 1 – 30 sts.
2nd size only: Next row: K. 2 tog., * k. 2, k. 2 tog.; rep. from * to last 6 sts., k. 6 – 34 sts.
For both sizes: Next row: Sl. 1, p. to last 2 sts., k. 2 tog.
Change to 3¾ mm. needles and in Bobble patt. work as follows:
Work 6 (8) rows, but dec. 1 st. at neck edge on every row – 23 (25) sts.
Cont. without shaping until armhole measures same as Back, ending with a wrong side row. Cast off rem. 23 (25) sts. in patt. With 4 mm. needles and wrong side facing, rejoin yarn to rem. 46 (50) sts. and in Cable patt. work as follows:
Next row: K. 1, patt. to last st., k. 1.
Work 6 rows, but dec. 1 st. at neck edge on every row – 40 (44) sts.
1st size only: Next row: Sl. 1, k. 2 tog., k. 1, * k. 2 tog., k. 2; rep. from * to end – 30 sts.
2nd size only: Next row: Sl. 1, k. 5, k. 2 tog., * k. 2, k. 2 tog.; rep. from * to end – 34 sts.
For both sizes: Next row: K. 2 tog., p. to last st., k. 1.
Change to 3¾ mm. needles and in Bobble patt. work as follows:
Work 6 (8) rows, but dec. 1 st. at neck edge on every row – 23 (25) sts. Cont. without shaping until armhole measures same as Back, ending with a wrong side row. Cast off rem. 23 (25) sts. in patt. Stitch up right shoulder seam.

Sleeves

With 3¼ mm. needles, cast on 55 (55) sts.
Row 1: Sl. 1, k. 1, * p. 1, k. 1; rep. from *

to last st., k. 1.
Row 2: Sl. 1, * p. 1, k. 1; rep. from * to end.
Rep. rows 1 and 2 until work measures 6 cm., ending on right side.
Next row: Inc. into next st., * inc. into next st. purlwise, inc. into next st.; rep. from * to end – 110 (110) sts.
Change to 4 mm. needles and work in Trellis patt. as given for Back until work measures 44 cm. from beg., ending with a wrong side row.

To shape top Cast off 1 st. in patt. at beg. of next 42 (50) rows. Cast off 2 sts. in patt. at beg. of next 20 (16) rows. Cast off rem. 28 sts. in patt.

Neckband

With 3¼ mm. needles and right side facing and beg. at top of left shoulder, pick up and k. 16 (17) sts. evenly along left side of front neck, 30 (34) sts. from cast off sts. at front neck, 16 (17) sts. along right side of front neck, 8 (10) sts. along right side of back neck, 29 (33) sts. from cast off sts. at back neck and 8 (10) sts. along left side of back neck – 107 (121) sts.
Row 1: Sl. 1, * p. 1, k. 1; rep. from * to end.
Row 2: Sl. 1, k. 1, * p. 1, k. 1; rep. from * to last st., k. 1.
Rep. rows 1 and 2 seven times, then row 1 once more, then cast off loosely rib-wise.

TO MAKE UP

Press according to instructions on ball band. Sew up left shoulder and neck-band seams. Fold neckband in half onto wrong side and sew in position. Set in sleeves. Sew up side and sleeve seams. Sew in shoulder pads.

Country Cousin

Very simple Aran jacket which can look chic or sporty. The chunky yarn and streamlined shape make it really quick to knit.
Very easy

MATERIALS

18 (19, 20) 50 g. balls Pingouin Pingoland *or* Pingouin Iceberg; a pair each 5½ mm. (no. 5) and 6 mm. (no. 4) knitting needles; four buttons; a cable needle.

TENSION

9 stitches and 14 rows to 7 cm. over reverse stocking stitch.

MEASUREMENTS

To fit bust 34 (36, 38) in., 86 (91, 96) cm.
Length 20½ (21, 21½) in., 52 (53, 54) cm.
Sleeve seam (all sizes) 17½ in., 45 cm.

ABBREVIATIONS

k., knit; p., purl; st(s)., stitch(es); alt., alternate; beg., beginning; cont., continue; dec., decrease; foll., following; g-st., garter stitch; inc., increas(e)(ing); patt., pattern; rem., remaining; rep., repeat; tog., together.

INSTRUCTIONS

Back

With 5½ mm. needles, cast on 66 (70, 74) sts. Work 18 rows in k. 2, p. 2 rib, inc. 6 sts. evenly along last row – 72 (76, 80) sts.
Change to 6 mm. needles and work patt. as follows:
Row 1: P. 13 (14, 15), k. 10, p. 26 (28, 30), k. 10, p. 13 (14, 15).
Row 2: K. the k. sts. and p. the p. sts. as they face you.
Rep. rows 1 and 2 twice more.
Row 7: P. 13 (14, 15), slip next 5 sts. onto a cable needle and leave at front of work, k. next 5 sts., then k. sts. from cable needle – called C5F – p. 26 (28, 30), slip next 5 sts. onto a cable needle and leave at back of work, k. next 5 sts.,

then k. 5 sts. from cable needle – called C5B – p. 13 (14, 15).
Row 8: As row 2.
Rows 9 to 14: Rep. rows 1 and 2 three times more.
These 14 rows form patt. When patt. has been worked three times in all, rep. rows 1 to 8 once more.

To shape armholes Keeping patt. correct, cast off 4 sts. at beg. of next 2 rows, then k. 2 tog. at beg. of next 6 rows – 58 (62, 66) sts.
Work straight until patt. has been completed six times in all, then work rows 1 to 4 (6, 8) (but do not twist cable for largest size) once more. Cast off.

Right front

With 5½ mm. needles, cast on 32 (36, 40) sts. Work 18 rows in k. 2, p. 2 rib, inc. 4 sts. evenly along last row – 36 (40, 44) sts.
Change to 6 mm. needles and work patt. as for Back, beg. as follows:
Row 1: P. 13 (15, 17), k. 10, p. 13 (15, 17), etc.
For this Front work C5B, and work C5F for Left Front.
When patt. has been worked three times in all, work rows 1 to 9 once more for Right Front and rows 1 to 8 for Left Front.

To shape armhole At outside edge, cast off 4 sts. at beg. of next row, then k. 2 tog. at same edge on next 3 alt. rows – 29 (31, 37) sts. At the same time, k. 2 tog. at neck edge on every foll. third row eleven (twelve, thirteen) times in all – 18 (21, 24) sts.
Complete to match length of Back. Cast off.

Left front

As Right Front, reversing shapings and cable.

Sleeves

With 5½ mm. needles, cast on 36 (38, 40) sts. Work in k. 2, p. 2 rib for 18 rows, inc. 4 sts. evenly along last row – 40 (42, 44) sts.
Change to 6 mm. needles and work patt. as for Back with first row as follows:
Row 1: P. 15 (16, 17), k. 10, p. 15 (16, 17). Work C5F for both sleeves, and inc. at each end of every tenth row until there are 50 (52, 54) sts. When length of sleeve is 45 cm. from beg., shape armholes.

To shape armholes Cast off 4 sts. at beg. of next 2 rows – 42 (44, 46) sts. Now k. 2 tog. at beg. of every row until 22 (24, 26) sts. remain. Cast off 3 sts. at beg. of next 4 rows. Cast off rem. sts.

Front bands and collar

With 5½ mm. needles, cast on 8 sts. and work 4 rows in g-st. (see page 13). Make a buttonhole by casting off the fifth st. from inside edge and casting it on again on next row. Make 4 buttonholes in all, each spaced 20 rows apart, then work band straight until length reaches along Right Front to beg. of neck shaping. Inc. 1 st. at inside edge on every third row to 15 sts., then work straight in g-st. until length reaches along right front and across half back neck.
Cont. to complete second half of collar as first half, reversing all shapings.

TO MAKE UP

Join shoulder seams. Set in sleeves. Join sleeve seams and side seams. Stitch on front bands and collar, positioning centre of collar at centre of back neck. Sew on buttons.

Cassata

Quick to knit pastel mohair cardigan in chevron stripes.
Easy

MATERIALS

2 40 g. balls Pingouin Mohair in each of green, white, yellow, blue and pink; a pair each 5 mm. (no. 6) and 6 mm. (no. 4) knitting needles; six buttons.

TENSION

13 stitches and 15 rows to 8 cm. square.

MEASUREMENTS

To fit bust 34-37 in., 86-94 cm. (actual size 39 in., 100 cm.)
Length 22¾ in., 58 cm.
Sleeve seam 17¾ in., 45 cm.

ABBREVIATIONS

k., knit; p., purl; st(s)., stitch(es); alt., alternate; beg., beginning; cont., continue; dec., decreas(e)(ing); foll., following; inc., increas(e)(ing); inc. 1 k., increase by picking up loop between sts. and knitting into back of it; patt., pattern; p.s.s.o., pass slip stitch over; rem., remaining; rep., repeat; sl., slip; st. st., stocking stitch; tog., together; y.f., yarn forward; A, green; B, white; C, yellow; D, blue; E, pink.

INSTRUCTIONS

Back

With 5 mm. needles and A, cast on 78 sts. Work 7 cm. in k. 2, p. 2 rib (1st row right side), beg. alt. rows p. 2 and inc. 1 st. at both ends of last row – 80 sts.
Break off A, change to 6 mm. needles and B. Cont. in patt. thus:
Rows 1 and 2: K.
Row 3: K. 2, (inc. 1 k., k. 4, sl. 1, k. 2 tog., p.s.s.o., k. 4, inc. 1 k., k. 2) to end.
Row 4: P.
Rows 5 to 12: Rep. rows 3 and 4 four times. These 12 rows form the patt. Cont. in patt., working 12 rows in each of C, D, E and B. The last 48 rows form the stripe sequence. Work should measure approx. 39 cm. *.

To shape armholes Keeping patt. and stripe sequence correct, cast off 4 sts. at beg. of next 2 rows, and 2 sts. at beg. of next 2 rows. Dec. 1 st. at both ends of next row and foll. alt. row – 64 sts.
Cont. straight until the second E stripe from beg. has been worked. Cast off.

Left front

With 5 mm. needles and A, cast on 50 sts. ** Work 7 cm. in rib as Back, ending after wrong side row.
Break off A. Change to 6 mm. needles and B.
Next row: K. 2 tog., k. to last 8 sts., sl. these 8 sts. onto a safety-pin.
Beg. with row 2, cont. in patt. as Back to *.

To shape armholes Cast off 4 sts. at beg. of next row, and 2 sts. at beg. of foll. alt. row. Dec. 1 st. at beg. of foll. 2 alt. rows – 33 sts.
Cont. straight until first row of second E stripe from beg. has been worked.

To shape neck Cast off 7 sts. at beg. of next row, and 4 sts. at beg. of foll. alt. row. Dec. 1 st. at neck edge on next 7 rows – 15 sts. Work 1 row. Cast off.

Right front

Work as Left Front to **. Work 2 cm. in rib as Back, ending after wrong side row.
Next row (buttonhole row): Rib 3, cast off 2 sts., rib to end.
Next row: In rib, casting on 2 sts. over those cast off. Cont. in rib until work measures 7 cm., ending after wrong side row.
Break off A. Change to 6 mm. needles.
Next row: Sl. first 8 sts. onto a safety-pin, join B, k. to last 2 sts., k. 2 tog. Complete to match Left Front, reversing shapings.

Sleeves

With 5 mm. needles and A, cast on 46 sts. Work 7 cm. in rib as Back, inc. 8 sts. evenly on last row – 54 sts.
Change to 6 mm. needles and beg. with E stripe, cont. in patt. and stripe sequence as Back until second B stripe has been worked. Sleeve should measure approx. 45 cm.

To shape top Cast off 4 sts. at beg. of next 2 rows. Dec. 1 st. at both ends of next row and foll. alt. rows until 20 sts. remain. Work 1 row straight. Cast off 4 sts. at beg. of next 2 rows. Cast off.

Front bands

With right side facing, sl. sts. from left front safety-pin onto 5 mm. needle. With A, cont. in rib until band, when slightly stretched, will fit up left front, ending after wrong side row. Leave sts. Mark band with pins to indicate buttons. Remembering that first one has been worked and placing last one 2 rows down from top, space rem. 4 equally between. Work right front band to match, working buttonholes as before at pin positions.

Neckband

Join shoulder seams, with right side facing, using 5 mm. needles and A, rib across sts. of right front band, pick up and k. 70 sts. round neck, rib across sts. of left front band. Work 7 rows in rib. Cast off ribwise.

TO MAKE UP

Do not press. Join side and sleeve seams. Sew in sleeves. Sew on front bands and buttons.

Colette

MATERIALS

9 (10) 100 g. balls Twilleys Pegasus 100% cotton, Twilleys Handicraft Cotton No. 1, *or* Twilleys Handicraft Cotton D. 42; a pair each 3¾ mm. (no. 9) and 4 mm. (no. 8) knitting needles; a cable needle.

TENSION

12 stitches and 16 rows to 5 cm. over pattern.

MEASUREMENTS

To fit bust 32-34 (36-38) in., 81-86 (91-97) cm. (actual size 36 (42) in., 91 (107) cm. all round)
Length 24½ (24¾) in., 62 (63) cm.
Sleeve (both sizes) 17 in., 43 cm.

ABBREVIATIONS

k., knit; p., purl; st(s)., stitch(es); alt., alternate; beg., beginning; cont., continue; C8F, place next 4 sts. on cable needle and hold at front of work, k. 4, then k. 4 from cable needle; dec., decrease; foll., following; inc., increase; patt., pattern; p.s.s.o., pass slip stitch over; rem., remaining; sep., separately; sl., slip; st. st., stocking stitch; tog., together; y.f., yarn forward.

INSTRUCTIONS

Back

With 3¾ mm. needles, cast on 90 (104) sts. Work 12 rows in k. 1, p. 1 rib.
Inc. row: Inc. into the ninth (tenth) and every foll. fourth st. to last 9 (10) sts., rib 9 (10) – 109 (126) sts.
Change to 4 mm. needles and work in patt. as follows:
Row 1: P. 8, (k. 8, p. 9) to last 16 sts., k. 8, p. 8.
Row 2: K. 8, (p. 8, k. 9) to last 16 sts., p. 8, k. 8.

Row 3: (K. 1, y.f., k. 1, sl. 1, k. 2 tog., p.s.s.o., k. 1, y.f., k. 1, p. 1, k. 8, p. 1) to last 7 sts., k. 1, y.f., k. 1, sl. 1, k. 2 tog., p.s.s.o., k. 1, y.f., k. 1.
Row 4: (P. 7, k. 1, p. 8, k. 1) to last 7 sts., p. 7.
Row 5: As row 3.
Row 6: As row 4.
Row 7: (K. 1, y.f., k. 1, sl. 1, k. 2 tog., p.s.s.o., k. 1, y.f., k. 1, p. 1, C8F, p. 1) to last 7 sts., k. 1, y.f., k. 1, sl. 1, k. 2 tog., p.s.s.o., k. 1, y.f., k. 1.
Rows 8, 10 and 16: As row 2.
Row 9: As row 1.
Rows 11, 13 and 15: As row 3.
Rows 12 and 14: As row 4.
These 16 rows form patt. Cont. in patt. until 7 repeats in all have been completed.

To shape armholes Cast off 6 sts. at beg. of next 2 rows, and 4 sts. at beg. of foll. 2 rows, then dec. 1 st. at each end of the foll. 3 alt. rows – 83 (100) sts. **.
Cont. in patt., working the extra sts. at each end of the row in st. st. (see page 13) until work measures 18 (19) cm. from beg. of armhole shaping.

To shape neck Work 28 (35), cast off centre 27 (29) sts., work to end. Finish each side sep.; dec. 1 st. at neck edge on every row until 24 (28) sts. remain. Cast off. Rejoin yarn and complete other side of the neck to match.

Front

As Back to **. Cont. in patt. until work measures 14 (15) cm. from beg. of armhole shaping.

To shape neck Work 31 (38), cast off centre 21 (23) sts., work 31 (38) sts. Finish each side sep. Dec. 1 st. at neck edge on every row until 24 (28) sts. remain. When length from beg. of arm-hole shaping matches that of Back, cast off. Rejoin yarn and complete other side of neck to match, reversing shaping.

Sleeves

With 3¾ mm. needles, cast on 46 sts. Work 12 rows in k. 1, p. 1 rib.
Inc. row: Inc. in every st. to end – 92 sts. Now work patt. as set for Back until work measures 43 cm. from beg.

To shape top Cast off 6 sts. at beg. of next 2 rows, and 4 sts. at beg. of foll. 2 rows, then dec. 1 st. at each end of every alt. row until 30 (26) sts. remain. Cast off 4 sts. at beg. of next 2 rows, cast off rem. sts.

Neckband

Join right shoulder seam. With 3¾ mm. needles, and right side facing, beg. at left neck edge, pick up and k. 54 (58) sts. along front neck and 42 (46) sts. along back neck edge. Work 7 rows in k. 1, p. 1 rib. Cast off ribwise.

TO MAKE UP

Join left shoulder seam and neckband. Set in sleeves. Join side and sleeve seams. Press all seams lightly.

Teddy Bear

MATERIALS

5 100 g. balls Laines Anny Blatt (Big'-Anny); 4 40 g. balls Laines Anny Blatt (Kid'Anny); a 12 mm. crochet hook; a fastener.

TENSION

Using Kid'Anny double: 5 h.tr. to 9 cm.; 4 h.tr. rows to 11 cm.

MEASUREMENTS

To fit bust 32-36 in., 81-91 cm.
Length 18½ in., 47 cm.
Sleeve 4¾ in., 12 cm.

ABBREVIATIONS

st(s)., stitch(es); beg., beginning; ch., chain; d.c., double crochet; h.tr., half treble; lp(s)., loop(s); patt., pattern; rep., repeat; tr., treble; y.r.h., yarn round hook; B.A., Big'Anny; K.A., Kid'Anny.

INSTRUCTIONS

Back
Beg. at sleeve edge and with 2 strands of K.A., make 18 ch.
Foundation row: Miss 1 ch., 1 d.c. in each ch. to end – 18 sts. Patt. thus:
Row 1 (wrong side): 1 ch., miss first d.c., (insert hook in next d.c., wind yarn over hook around 3 fingers of left hand and over hook again and draw 2 lps. through, y.r.h. and draw through all 3 lps. – lp. st. worked) to end, 1 d.c. in 1 ch.
Row 2: 1 ch., miss first d.c., 1 d.c. in each st. to end, 1 d.c. in 1 ch.
Rep. rows 1 and 2 twice more, then row 1 again. These 8 rows complete sleeve. Break off K.A.; join B.A.
Row 9: 2 ch., miss first st., 1 h.tr. in each st. to end, 1 h.tr. in top of ch. *.
Rep. row 9 sixteen times more. Break off B.A. Join 2 strands K.A. Work sleeve.

Next row: 1 ch., miss first h.tr., lp. st. in each h.tr. to end, 1 d.c. in top of ch. Work row 2 of first sleeve. Rep. rows 1 and 2 three times more. Fasten off.

Right front
Work as Back to *. Rep last row once more. Break off B.A. Join 2 strands of K.A.
Next row: As row 2 of Back. Rep. rows 1 and 2 of Back three times more, then row 1 again **. Break off K.A. Join B.A.
Next 2 rows: 2 ch., miss first st., 1 h.tr. in 10 sts., turn. Fasten off.

Left front
As Right Front to **. Break off K.A.
Next row: Join B.A. to eighth st., 2 ch., 1 h.tr. in 9 sts., 1 h.tr. in top of ch. Work 1 row h.tr. Fasten off.

Lower band
With right sides facing, join B.A. to lower end of last row of left front, 2 ch., work 13 h.tr. across ends of rows omitting sleeve edge, then omitting sleeve edges work 22 h.tr. across lower edge of back and 14 h.tr. across lower edge of right front, ending at last row of front. Work 5 rows h.tr. Fasten off.

TO MAKE UP

Join upper sleeve and shoulder seams. Join underarm seams. Sew on fastener.

Woolly Lamb

MATERIALS

4 100 g. balls Laines Anny Blatt (Boucl'Anny); 3 80 g. balls Mel'Anny; a pair 7½ mm. (no. 1) knitting needles; five buttons; a stitch-holder.

TENSION

Using Mel'Anny double: 9 stitches and 17 rows to 10 cm. over reversed stocking stitch.

MEASUREMENTS

To fit bust 32-38 in., 81-97 cm.
Length 19¾ in., 50 cm.

ABBREVIATIONS

k., knit; p., purl; st(s)., stitch(es); beg., beginning; cont., continue; dec., decreas(e)(ing); foll., following; inc., increas(e)(ing); m. 1, make one; patt., pattern; p.s.s.o., pass slip stitch over; rem., remaining; rep., repeat; sl., slip; st. st., stocking stitch; t.b.l., through back of loop; y.fd., yarn forward; B.A., Boucl'Anny; M.A., Mel'Anny.

INSTRUCTIONS

Back

With B.A., cast on 33 sts. K. 6 rows.
Inc. row: K. 2, (pick up strand lying between needles and k. it t.b.l. – referred to as m. 1 – k. 4) to end, ending last rep. k. 3 – 41 sts.
Beg. p. (right side), cont. in reversed st. st. (see page 13), inc. 1 st. at each end of fifteenth and every foll. third row until there are 59 sts. K. 1 row, thus ending with a wrong side row. Break off B.A.; join 2 strands of M.A. *. Patt thus:
Row 1 (right side): P. 2, (sl. 1, p. 2, p.s.s.o. 2 p. sts.) to end.
Row 2: K. 2, (y.fd., k. 2) to end.
Row 3: P. 1, (sl. 1, p. 2, p.s.s.o. 2 p. sts.) to last st., p. 1.
Row 4: K. 1, (y.fd., k. 2) to last st., k. 1.

Knitted jerkin in bouclé yarn with insets of texture.
Easy

These 4 rows form patt. *. Rep. 4 patt. rows twice more.
Break off M.A. Join B.A. Beg. p., work 18 rows in reversed st. st. Cast off.

Left front

With B.A., cast on 19 sts. K. 6 rows.
Inc. row: K. 3, (m. 1, k. 4) to end – 23 sts.
Beg. p., work 10 rows in reversed st. st. **.
Pocket opening row: P. 10, turn; cont. on these sts. only.
Next row: Cast on 12 sts., k. to end. Cont. inc. 1 st. at beg. (side edge) of third row and at this edge on every foll. third row until there are 27 sts. Work 1 row.
Next row: P. to last 12 sts., cast off 12. Leave sts. on a stitch-holder. With right side facing, rejoin yarn at inner end of rem. 13 sts. Work 19 rows.
Next row: K. 13, then from stitch-holder, k. 14, inc. in last st. Cont. inc. at side edge on every third row until there are 32 sts. Work 1 row. Break off B.A. Join 2 strands M.A. Rep. from * to * of Back

three times. Break off M.A. Join B.A. P. 1 row. Cont. in reversed st. st., dec. 1 st. at beg. of next row and at this edge on foll. 17 rows – 14 sts. Break off B.A. Join 2 strands of M.A. Rep. from * to * of Back twice. Cast off.

Right front

As Left Front to **.
Pocket opening row: P. 13, turn. Cont. on these sts. only. Work 18 rows. Leave sts. on a stitch-holder. With right side facing, rejoin yarn at inner end of rem. 10 sts., cast on 12 sts., p. to end. Cont. inc. 1 st. at end (side edge) of fourth row and at this edge on every foll. third row until there are 27 sts. Work 1 row. Cast off 12 sts. at beg. of next row.
Next row: Inc. in first st., k. 14, k. 13 sts. from stitch-holder. Complete as Left Front, reversing shapings.

Neckband

Join shoulder seams. Using 2 strands of M.A., pick up and k. 75 sts. evenly around neck. K. 5 rows. Cast off.

Armbands

Work as neckband, beg. and ending 24 cm. from shoulder seams and pick up and k. 52 sts. along sides of main part.

Front bands

With right side facing and using 2 strands of M.A., pick up and k. 50 sts. up right front edge. K. 2 rows.
Next row (make buttonholes): K. 2, (y.fd., k. 2 tog., k. 8) four times, y.fd., k. 2 tog., k. 6.
K. 2 rows. Cast off. Work other band to match, omitting buttonholes.

Pocket edges

Work as neckband, picking up 14 sts. along edge of pocket.

TO MAKE UP

Press lightly. Join side and armband seams. Sew down pocket linings and ends of pocket edges. Sew on buttons.

Ginger

MATERIALS

14 (15, 16) 50 g. balls Pingouin Pingoland or Pingouin Iceberg; a pair each 5 mm. (no. 6) and 6 mm. (no. 4) knitting needles; a cable needle.

TENSION

7 stitches and 9 rows to 5 cm. over pattern; 18 stitches (1 complete pattern) to 11 cm.

MEASUREMENTS

To fit bust 34 (36, 38) in., 86 (91, 97) cm.
Length 21½ (22, 22½) in., 55 (56, 57) cm.
Sleeve (all sizes) 16½ in., 42 cm.

ABBREVIATIONS

k., knit; p., purl; st(s)., stitch(es); beg., beginning; cont., continue; C3B, cable 3 back; C3F, cable 3 forward; dec., decrease; inc., increase; patt., pattern; p.s.s.o., pass slip stitch over; rem., remaining; rep., repeat; sl., slip; tog., together; y.fd., yarn forward.

INSTRUCTIONS

Back

With 5 mm. needles, cast on 67 (71, 75) sts. Work 10 rows in k. 1, p. 1 rib, beg. second row p. 1.
Change to 6 mm. needles and patt. thus:
Row 1 (wrong side): K. 13 (15, 17), (* p. 2, k. 1, p. 2 *, k. 13) to end, k. 0 (2, 4).
Row 2: P. 13 (15, 17), (* sl. next 3 sts. onto cable needle and leave at back, k. 2, then over sts. from cable needle p. 1, k. 2 *, p. 13) to last 0 (2, 4) sts., p. 0 (2, 4).
Row 3: As row 1.
Row 4: P. 12 (14, 16), (* sl. next st. onto cable needle and leave at back, k. 2, p. st. from cable needle – referred to as C3B – k. 1, sl. next 2 sts. onto cable

---

needle and leave at front, p. 1, k. sts. from cable needle – referred to as C3F – * p. 11) to last 1 (3, 5) sts., p. 1 (3, 5).
Row 5: K. 12 (14, 16), (p. 2, k. 1, p. 1, k. 1, p. 2, k. 11) to last 1 (3, 5) sts., k. 1 (3, 5).
Row 6: P. 11 (13, 15), (C3B, k. 1, p. 1, k. 1, C3F, p. 9) to last 2 (4, 6) sts., p. 2 (4, 6).
Row 7: K. 11 (13, 15), * p. 2, (k. 1, p. 1) twice, k. 1, p. 2, k. 9; rep. from * to last 2 (4, 6) sts., k. 2 (4, 6).
Row 8: P. 10 (12, 14), * C3B, (k. 1, p. 1) twice, k. 1, C3F, p. 7; rep. from * to last 3 (5, 7) sts., p. 3 (5, 7).
Row 9: K. 10 (12, 14), * p. 2, (k. 1, p. 1) three times, k. 1, p. 2, k. 7; rep. from * to last 3 (5, 7) sts., k. 3 (5, 7).
Row 10: P. 9 (11, 13), * C3B, (k. 1, p. 1) three times, k. 1, C3F, p. 5; rep. from * to last 4 (6, 8) sts., p. 4 (6, 8).
Row 11: K. 9 (11, 13), * p. 2, (k. 1, p. 1) four times, k. 1, p. 2, k. 5; rep. from * to last 4 (6, 8) sts., k. 4 (6, 8).
Row 12: P. 9 (11, 13), * C3F, (p. 1, k. 1) three times, p. 1, C3B, p. 5; rep. from * to last 4 (6, 8) sts., p. 4 (6, 8).
Row 13: As row 9.
Row 14: P. 10 (12, 14), * C3F, (p. 1, k. 1) twice, p. 1, C3B, p. 7; rep. from * to last 3 (5, 7) sts., p. 3 (5, 7).
Row 15: As row 7.
Row 16: P. 11 (13, 15), (C3F, p. 1, k. 1, p. 1, C3B, p. 9) to last 2 (4, 6) sts., p. 2 (4, 6).
Row 17: As row 5.
Row 18: P. 12 (14, 16), (C3F, p. 1, C3B, p. 11) to last 1 (3, 5) sts., p. 1 (3, 5).
Row 19: As row 1.
Row 20: As row 2.
Row 21: As row 1.
Row 22: P. 12 (14, 16), (C3B, p. 1, C3F, p. 11) to last 1 (3, 5) sts., p. 1 (3, 5).
Row 23: K. 12 (14, 16), (p. 2, k. 3, p. 2, k. 11) to last 1 (3, 5) sts., k. 1 (3, 5).

Row 24: P. 11 (13, 15), (C3B, p. 3, C3F, p. 9) to last 2 (4, 6) sts., p. 2 (4, 6).
Row 25: K. 11 (13, 15), (p. 2, k. 5, p. 2, k. 9) to last 2 (4, 6) sts., k. 2 (4, 6).
Row 26: P. 11 (13, 15), * k. 2, p. 2, then (k. 1, y.fd.) in next st. twice, k. 1, turn; p. 5, turn; k. 5, turn; p. 2 tog., p. 1, p. 2 tog., turn; sl. 1, k. 2 tog., p.s.s.o. – bobble made, p. 2, k. 2, p. 9; rep. from * to last 2 (4, 6) sts., p. 2 (4, 6).
Row 27: As row 25.
Row 28: P. 11 (13, 15), (C3F, p. 3, C3B, p. 9) to last 2 (4, 6) sts., p. 2 (4, 6).
Row 29: As row 23.
Row 30: As row 18.
These 30 rows form patt. Rep. rows 1 to 21 once.

To shape armhole Cont. in patt. as set but cast off 5 sts. at beg. of next 2 rows. Dec. 1 st. at each end of next 2 rows – 53 (57, 61) sts.
** Cont. until first (third, fifth) row of fourth patt. has been completed. Cast off.

Front

As Back to **. Cont. until row 20 of third patt. has been completed.

To shape neck Next row: Patt. 17 (19, 21), cast off centre 19 sts., patt. 17 (19, 21). Cont. on last sts. only. Dec. 1 st. at neck edge on next 4 rows. Patt. 6 (8, 10) rows. Cast off. Rejoin yarn to inner end of rem. sts. and complete other side to match.

Sleeves

With 5 mm. needles, cast on 38 (40, 42) sts. Work 10 rows in k. 1, p. 1 rib.
Inc. row: Rib 4 (3, 2), * inc. in next st., rib 6 (7, 8); rep. from * to end, ending last rep. rib 5 (4, 3) – 43 (45, 47) sts.
Change to 6 mm. needles and work centre patt. panel thus:
Row 1 (wrong side): K. 19 (20, 21); rep. from * to * of first patt. row of Back, k. 19 (20, 21).
Row 2: P. 19 (20, 21); rep. from * to * of second row of Back, p. 19 (20, 21).
Row 3: As row 1.
Row 4: P. 18 (19, 20); rep. from * to * of fourth row of Back, p. 18 (19, 20). Beg. with fifth row, cont. with centre patt.

Modern Aran classic in diamond and bobble pattern with a crew neck. The chunky yarn is lovely to work with, and the pattern is enjoyable if you have just learnt how to do Aran.

panel as set but inc. 1 st. at each end of second and every foll. tenth row until there are 53 (55, 57) sts. Cont. straight until work measures 42 cm. from beg., ending with seventh row of third patt.

To shape top Cast off 5 sts. at beg. of next 2 rows. Dec. 1 st. at beg. of every row until 25 sts. remain. Cast off 3 sts. at beg. of next 4 rows. Cast off loosely.

Neckband

Join right shoulder. With 5 mm. needles and right side facing, pick up and k. 68 sts. around neck, leaving 13 (15, 17) sts. for left shoulder. Work 5 rows in k. 1, p. 1 rib. Cast off ribwise.

TO MAKE UP

Join left shoulder and neckband seam. Set in sleeves. Join side and sleeve seams. Press seams lightly.

Madame Butterfly

MATERIALS

4 (5, 5) 50 g. balls Patons Clansman D.K. in main shade – black and 1 ball in each of 5 contrast shades – green, pink, yellow, brick and red; a pair each 4 mm. (no. 8) and 4½ mm. (no. 7) knitting needles.

TENSION

10 stitches and 13 rows to 5 cm.

MEASUREMENTS

To fit bust 32 (34, 36) in., 81 (86, 91) cm. loosely
Length (all sizes) 21¼ in., 54 cm.
Sleeve (all sizes) 16½ in., 42 cm.

NOTE ON MOTIF KNITTING

When working a single motif, use a separate ball of yarn for each section and twist yarns on wrong side as you change colour to avoid leaving a hole.

Jacquard sweater with butterfly and flower motif, suitable for knitters who have just learnt how to work from a chart.

ABBREVIATIONS

k., knit; p., purl; st(s)., stitch(es); alt., alternate; beg., beginning; cont., continue; dec., decrease; g-st., garter stitch; inc., increase; patt., pattern; rep., repeat; st. st., stocking stitch; tog., together; y.fd., yarn forward; MS, main shade (black); G, green; Y, yellow.

INSTRUCTIONS

Back

With 4 mm. needles and MS, cast on 90 (94, 98) sts. Work 10 cm. in k. 2, p. 2 rib, beg. second row p. 2 and for 3rd size inc. 1 st. at each end of last row.
Change to 4½ mm. needles *. Beg. k., cont. in st. st. (see page 13) until work measures 52.5 cm., ending with a p. row.

To shape neck Next row: K. 21 (22, 24), turn. Cont. on these sts. only. Dec. 1 st. at neck edge on next 3 rows. Cast off. Rejoin yarn, cast off centre 48 (50, 52) sts. and work other side to match.

Front

As Back to *. Beg. k., work 12 rows in st. st. Cont. in st. st., working motif patt. from chart 1 (see Note left) thus:
Row 1: K. 5 (7, 10) MS then reading row 1 of chart from right to left, k. 41 MS, 1 G, 30 MS across sts. of chart, then k. 13 (15, 18) MS.
Row 2: P. 13 (15, 18) MS, then reading row 2 of chart from left to right p. 30 MS, 3 G, 39 MS across sts. of chart, then p. 5 (7, 10) MS. Complete chart 1 in this way, reading k. rows from right to left and p. rows from left to right, working colours as key and noting that dark symbol of pink is worked in reversed st. st. (see page 13), still twisting yarns on wrong side. Cont. with MS and work 12 rows. Now work motif patt. from chart 2 (see Note left) thus:
Row 1: K. 21 (23, 26) MS, then reading row 1 of chart from right to left k. 6 MS, 1 Y, 28 MS across sts. of chart, then k. 34 (36, 39) MS.
Row 2: P. 34 (36, 39) MS, then reading row 2 of chart from left to right p. 27 MS,

Chart 1

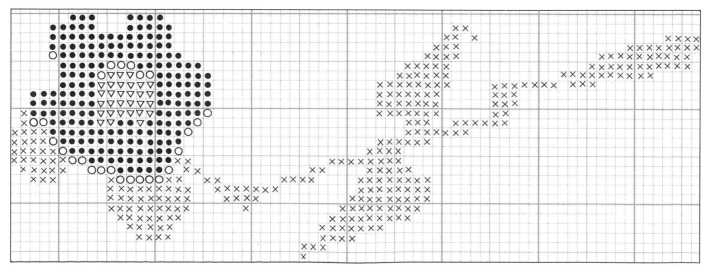

□ Main colour   × Green   ○ Pink   ● Pink reversed   ▽ Yellow

1 Y, and MS across sts. of chart, then p. 21 (23, 26) MS. Complete chart 2 as set, working as for chart 1, but noting that dark symbol of yellow is worked in reversed st. st. Cont. with MS only and work 4 rows.

To shape neck *Next row:* K. 25 (26, 28), turn. Cont. on these sts. only. Dec. 1 st. at beg. of next and every alt. row until 18 (19, 21) sts. remain. Cont. until work measures 54 cm. Cast off. Cast off centre 40 (42, 44) sts. and work other side to match.

Neckband

Join right shoulder seam. With 4 mm. needles and right side facing and with MS, pick up and k. 68 (70, 72) sts. around front neck and 56 (58, 60) sts. around back neck. Work 8 rows in k. 2, p. 2 rib. Cast off.

Armbands

Join left shoulder and neckband seam. Beg. and ending 26 cm. from shoulder seam and picking up 96 sts. from side of back and front, work as neckband.

TO MAKE UP

Press work. Join side and armband seams.

Chart 2

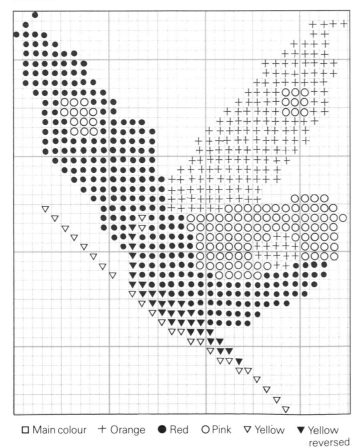

□ Main colour + Orange ● Red ○ Pink ▽ Yellow ▼ Yellow reversed

Double Take

MATERIALS

17 (18, 19) 25 g. balls Twilleys Gold-fingering (bronze); a pair each 3 mm. (no. 11) and 3¼ mm. (no. 10) knitting needles; six round buttons.

TENSION

28 stitches and 46 rows to 9 cm.

MEASUREMENTS

To fit bust 34 (36, 38) in., 86 (91, 97) cm.
Length 23½ (24, 24½) in., 60 (61, 62) cm.
Sleeve (all sizes) 15½ in., 40 cm.

ABBREVIATIONS

k., knit; p., purl; st(s)., stitch(es); alt., alternate; beg., beginning; cont., continue; dec(s)., decrease(s); foll., following; inc., increas(e)(ing); m. 1, make one; patt., pattern; p.s.s.o., pass slip stitch over; rep., repeat; sl., slip; st. st., stocking stitch, t.b.l., through back of loop; tog., together; y.r.n., yarn round needle.

INSTRUCTIONS

Beg. at bottom Left Front. With 3 mm. needles, cast on 70 (76, 84) sts. Work in k. 1, p. 1 rib for 5 cm., inc. 1 st. at end of last rib row for 2nd size only and ending with a wrong side row – 70 (77, 84) sts.
Change to 3¼ mm. needles and work the foll. patt.:
Row 1: * K. 2, k. 2 tog., y.r.n. to m. 1, k. 3 *; rep. from * to * to end.
Row 2: * P. 1, p. 2 tog. t.b.l., m. 1, p. 1, m. 1, p. 2 tog., p. 1 *; rep. from * to * to end.
Row 3: * K. 2 tog., m. 1, k. 3, m. 1, sl. 1, k. 1, p.s.s.o. *; rep. from * to * to end.
Rows 4 and 8: P.
Row 5: * M. 1, sl. 1, k. 1, p.s.s.o., k. 5 *; rep. from * to * to end.
Row 6: * M. 1, p. 2 tog., p. 2, p. 2 tog. t.b.l., m. 1, p. 1 *; rep. from * to * to end.
Row 7: * K. 2, m. 1, sl. 1, k. 1, p.s.s.o., k.

2 tog., m. 1, k. 1 *; rep. from * to * to end.
These 8 rows form patt. Work patt. until work measures 36 cm. from beg.

To shape neck and sleeve At outside edge, inc. 1 st. on every row fourteen times in all, working the extra sts. in st. st. (see page 13) until 1 patt. (7 sts.) has been completed, making two further patts. in all. At the same time, at neck edge, dec. 1 st. on the next and every foll. fourth row. While working these decs., mark the end of the first patt. and work it in st. st. until 7 decs. have been worked, then mark end of next patt., working decs. in the same way.
When 14 patt. rows have been completed from the beg. of sleeve shaping, cont. to shape neck as set, but at outer edge cast on 21 sts. on the next and foll. 2 alt. rows – 142 (149, 156) sts.
Cont. to shape neck, working straight at sleeve edge until length at sleeve edge measures 19 (20, 21) cm. and 118 (123, 129) sts. remain.
Mark row at each end to show beg. of Back.

To shape back neck Work 3 patts. straight. Now inc. 1 st. on every row

fourteen times in all. Leave these sts. for the time being.

Right front

Exactly as Left Front, reversing all shapings, and ending on same patt. row.

To shape back At inside edge of Right Front, cast on 35 sts. and join to Left Front, work to end – 299 (309, 321) sts. Work straight in patt. until work measures 19 (20, 21) cm. from marked row.

To complete sleeve shaping Cast off 21 sts. at beg. of next 6 rows – 173 (183, 195) sts.
Dec. 1 st. at each end of next 14 rows – 145 (155, 167) sts.
Complete Back to match length of Front to beg. of rib. Change to 3 mm. needles and work in k. 1, p. 1 rib for 5 cm. Cast off ribwise.

Front band

With 3 mm. needles, cast on 12 sts. Work in k. 1, p. 1 rib for 9 rows.
Buttonhole row: Rib 5, cast off 2, rib to end.
Next row: Rib 5, cast on 2, rib to end.
Work 5 further buttonholes, each spaced 22 rows apart, then work in rib without buttonholes to fit entire inner edge.

Sleeve bands

With 3 mm. needles and right side facing, pick up and k. 78 (86, 94) sts. along left sleeve edge. Work in k. 1, p. 1 rib for 10 cm. then cast off ribwise. Work band of right sleeve to match.

Cover buttons to match (*six the same*)

Work the foll. cover for each button. With 3 mm. needles, cast on 3 sts. Now work in st. st. but inc. 1 st. at each end of every row until there are 12 sts. Now dec. 1 st. at each end of every row until 3 sts. remain. Cast off. Gather each cover over a button and stitch down.

TO MAKE UP

Join sleeve seams and side seams. Sew on front band. Sew on buttons to correspond. Press seams according to instructions on ball band.

Geisha

10 (11, 12) 50 g. balls Pingouin Type Shetland 100% Laine in main shade – Noir; 1 25 g. ball Twilleys Goldfingering in contrast shade – silver; 1 skein Twilleys Lystra Stranded Embroidery Cotton in each of light jade (no. 713) and medium jade (no. 714), 2 skeins in each of dark jade (no. 715), light pink (no. 512), medium pink (no. 513), dark pink (no. 514) and light mauve (no. 540), and 3 skeins in each of medium mauve (no. 539) and dark mauve (no. 538); a pair 3¾ mm. (no. 9) knitting needles; a 3¾ mm. (no. 9) circular knitting needle; 20 cm. medium weight Terylene wadding for the borders.

TENSION

12 stitches and 15 rows to 5 cm.

MEASUREMENTS

To fit bust 34 (36, 38) in., 86 (91, 97) cm.
Length 24½ (25, 25½) in., 61.5 (63, 64.5) cm.
Sleeve (all sizes) 16½ in., 42 cm.

ABBREVIATIONS

k., knit; p., purl; st(s)., stitch(es); alt., alternate; beg., beginning; cont., continue; dec., decreas(e)(ing); foll., following; inc., increas(e)(ing); lp(s)., loop(s); rep., repeat; st. st., stocking stitch; t.b.l., through back of loop; tog., together; MS, main shade (black); CS, contrast shade (silver).

INSTRUCTIONS

Back

With MS, cast on 110 (116, 122) sts. Beg. k., work in st. st. (see page 13), inc. 1 st. at each end of fifth and every foll. sixth row until there are 118 (124, 130)

Embroidered evening coat makes an Oriental connection. The jacket is knitted in stocking stitch with quilted, padded borders and hems, then embroidered in chain stitch in embroidery silks and silver yarn.

sts. Cont. straight until work measures 38 cm., ending with a p. row.

To shape armhole Cast off 5 sts. at beg. of next 2 rows. Dec. 1 st. at each end of every foll. third row until 98 (104, 110) sts. remain, then dec. 1 st. at each end of every fourth row until 84 (88, 92) sts. remain. P. 1 row.

To shape neck Next row: K. 31 (32, 33), turn. Work 6 rows, dec. 1 st. at neck edge on first 4 of these rows and at the same time dec. 1 st. at beg. of second and last row at armhole. Work 3 rows straight. Cast off. With right side facing, rejoin yarn at inner end of remaining sts., cast off centre 22 (24, 26) sts., k. to end. Complete to match other side, reversing shapings.

Right front

With MS, cast on 37 (40, 43) sts. K. 1 row, p. 1 row. Inc. 1 st. at beg. of next and every alt. row and at the same time inc. 1 st. at end of third and every foll. sixth row until there are 52 (55, 58) sts. Cont. inc. 1 st. at beg. of every alt. row (front edge) only until there are 59 (62, 65) sts. Cont. straight until work measures 34 cm., ending with a k. row.

To shape front Dec. 1 st. at end of next row and at this edge on every third row until 55 (58, 61) sts. remain *. Work 2 rows.

To shape armhole Next row: Cast off 5 sts., p. to last 2 sts., p. 2 tog. **. Dec. 1 st. at each end of every foll. third row until 39 (42, 45) sts. remain, then dec. 1 st. at each end of every foll. fourth row until 29 (30, 31) sts. remain. Dec. 1 st. at armhole edge only on every foll. fourth row until 25 (26, 27) sts. remain. Work 3 rows. Cast off.

Left front

Reversing shapings by reading beg. for end and end for beg., work as Right Front to *. Work 1 row.

To shape armhole Cast off 5 sts. at beg. of next row. Dec. 1 st. at beg. of next row. Complete as Right Front from **.

Sleeves

Cut 6 strips of wadding 32 (34, 36) cm. long and 2.5 cm. wide. With MS and using the two-needle method, cast on 72 (78, 84) sts. Beg. k., work 6 rows in st. st. *. Break off MS, join CS and k. 1 row. Break off CS, join MS, beg. p., work 5 rows in st. st. *. Rep. from * to * once more. K. 1 row. K. t.b.l. 1 row (hemline) **. Beg. k., work 8 rows in st. st. Folding work wrong sides tog. along hemline, lay a strip of wadding in fold and enclose thus:
Tuck row: Insert needle in first st. and through first lp. of second row worked in CS and k. both lps. tog. (k. next st. and next lp. tog.) to end **. Beg. p., work 7 rows in st. st. Lay another strip of wadding across wrong side of work and enclose in the same way but to work tuck

row, k. each st. tog. with corresponding lp. of first row worked in CS. Rep. last 8 rows again, but to work tuck row, k. each st. tog. with corresponding lp. of cast-on edge. Beg p., cont. in st. st. until work measures 42 cm. from hemline, ending with a p. row.

To shape top Cast off 5 sts. at beg. of next 2 rows. Dec. 1 st. at beg. of every row until 24 sts. remain. Cast off 4 sts. at beg. of next 4 rows. Cast off.

Borders (*two*)

Cut wadding into strips 2.5 cm. wide. With circular needle and using the two-needle method, cast on 226 (236, 246) sts. Beg. k., work 6 rows in st. st. Work as Sleeve from * to *. K. 1 row. K. t.b.l. 1 row (hemline). Work as Sleeve from ** to **, working tuck row into the row worked in CS. Beg. p., work 7 rows in st. st. Cast off. Trim ends of the wadding.

TO MAKE UP

Press work.

Embroidery: Using silver, work horizontal zigzag chain stitch (see diagram 1) along for branches as shown in layout diagram, working 1 or 2 lines more parallel to first at thicker areas and building rows of 2 or 3 sts. over each other for vertical branches. Take care to match designs so that right front will butt with back design and left sleeve with left front design at shoulder. Work flowers in 3 shades of pink and 3 shades of mauve as

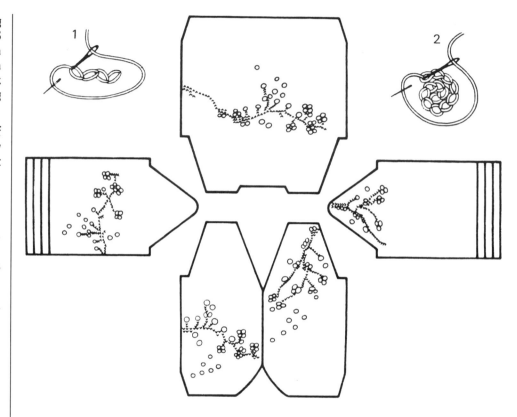

indicated. Beg. with lightest shade at centre working outwards in spiral of chain stitch (see diagram 2) changing shades to finish with darkest. Work oval-shaped leaves in the same way in green shades. Join shoulder seams. Set in sleeves. Join side and sleeve seams. Join ends of borders. Placing seams to centre

back of neck and lower edge with right sides tog., sew cast-off edge of border around entire outer edge. Place strips of wadding inside tuck and sew cast-on edge down over wrong side of seam. Press seams. With silver, zigzag chain stitch over contrast row inside cuffs and front border.

Blazing Saddles

INSTRUCTIONS

Jacket

Back

With 6½ mm. needles, cast on 61 (64, 67) sts. Beg. with a k. row, work in st. st. (see page 13) for 5 rows.

This jacket, with saddle shoulders, cabled sleeves and hems instead of rib, is knitted in a luxury yarn: a mix of pure wool and mohair.
Easy

Next row: Instead of purling, k. each st. t.b.l. to mark hemline.
Change to 7½ mm. needles. Beg. with a k. row, work in st. st. until work measures 42 cm.

To shape armholes Cont. to work in st. st. but dec. 1 st. at beg. of next 10 rows – 51 (54, 57) sts. Now work 8 rows straight in st. st. Dec. 1 st. at each end of next 6 rows – 39 (42, 45) sts. Cast off 8 sts. at beg. of next 2 rows – 23 (26, 29) sts. Cast off rem. sts.

Right front

With 6½ mm. needles, cast on 28 (30, 32) sts. Beg. with a k. row, work in st. st. for 5 rows.

Next row: Instead of purling, k. each st. t.b.l. to mark hemline.
Change to 7½ mm. needles. Beg. with a k. row, work in st. st. until work measures 13 cm. from hemline. Leave these sts. for the time being.

Pocket linings

With 7½ mm. needles, cast on 15 sts. Work in st. st. for 18 rows, ending with a p. row. Do not cast off.

To work pocket opening Return to Right Front. K. 9 (11, 13), (p. 1, k. 1) seven times, p. 1, k. 4.
Next row: P. 4 (k. 1, p. 1) seven times, k. 1, p. 9 (11, 13).
Rep. these 2 rows once more.
Next row: K. 9 (11, 13), cast off the next 15 sts., k. over the 15 sts. of Pocket Lining in place of cast off sts., k. to end. Cont. in st. st. until work measures 42 cm. from beg., ending with a p. row.

To shape neck Dec. 1 st. at neck edge on next and every foll. third row. After first dec. at neck edge, work 1 row, then shape armhole.

To shape armhole At armhole edge, dec. 1 st. on next and foll. 4 alt. rows. Cont. to shape neck as set, but now work 8 rows straight at armhole edge. Now dec. 1 st. at armhole edge on the next 8 rows. Cast off rem. 7 (9, 11) sts.

Left front

Exactly as Right Front, reversing all shapings.

Sleeves

With 6½ mm. needles, cast on 31 (33, 35) sts. Work in k. 1, p. 1 rib for 10 rows, working 7 incs. evenly along last rib row – 38 (40, 42) sts.
Change to 7½ mm. needles and work the foll. cable patt.:
Row 1: K. 13 (14, 15), p. 2, k. 8, p. 2, k. 13 (14, 15).
Row 2: K. the k. sts. and p. the p. sts. as they face you.
Rep. rows 1 and 2 twice more.
Row 7: K. 13 (14, 15), p. 2, C4F, p. 2, k. 13 (14, 15).
Row 8: As row 2.

Rep. rows 1 and 2 twice more. These 12 rows form patt. Cont. to work this patt. until work measures 18 cm. from beg. Now inc. 1 st. at each end of next and every foll. eighth row while still working cable until there are 50 (52, 54) sts. and work measures 44 cm. from beg.

To shape armholes Dec. 1 st. at the beg. of the next 18 rows – 32 (34, 36) sts. Now dec. 1 st. at each end of every row until 18 sts. remain. Patt. 6 rows straight for saddle shoulder extension, working 4 decs. over cable on last row – 14 sts. Cast off 7 sts., work to end. Work 1 row. Cast off rem. 7 sts.

Front band
With 6½ mm. needles, cast on 10 sts. Work in k. 1, p. 1 rib for 6 rows.
Buttonhole row: Rib 4, cast off next 2 sts., rib to end.
Next row: Rib 4, cast on 2 sts., rib to end. Cont. in k. 1, p. 1 rib, working 3 more buttonholes, each spaced 14 rows apart. Now work in k. 1, p. 1 rib without button-holes until length of band fits entire inner edge. Cast off.

TO MAKE UP

Set in sleeves. Stitch saddle extensions to the 8 sts. cast off at either side of top of back and to cast-off edges of fronts. Join sleeve seams and side seams. Stitch down pocket linings. Stitch down hems at bottom of garment on the inside. Sew on front band. Sew on buttons. Press all seams.

Anklewarmers

Cast on 32 (36, 40) sts. and arrange them on 3 of the 4 needles. Now work in rounds of k. 1, p. 1 rib until work measures 32 (33, 34) cm. from beg. Cast off ribwise.

Indian Summer

Vivid cotton sweater with short sleeves and a Fair Isle yoke, in five contrast shades.
Easy Fair Isle

MATERIALS

6 (6, 7, 7) 50 g. balls Twilleys Stalite in main shade (no. 21 – natural) and 1 ball in each of contrast shades (no. 9 – rust, no. 30 – pink, no. 27 – gold, no. 37 – dark brown and no. 22 – beige); a pair each 2¾ mm. (no. 12) and 3 mm. (no. 11) knitting needles; a 3 mm. (no. 11) circular knitting needle.

TENSION

14 stitches and 18 rows to 5 cm. over stocking stitch.

MEASUREMENTS

To fit bust 32 (34, 36, 38) in., 81 (86, 91, 97) cm.
Length 22 (22½, 22¾, 23¼) in., 56 (57, 58, 59) cm.
Sleeve 6¾ (7, 7, 7½) in., 17 (18, 18, 19) cm.

ABBREVIATIONS

k., knit; p., purl; st(s)., stitch(es); alt., alternate; beg., beginning; dec., decrease; foll., following; inc., increase; p.s.s.o., pass slip stitch over; rem., remaining; rep., repeat; sl., slip; st. st., stocking stitch; tog., together; MS, main shade (natural).

INSTRUCTIONS

Back and front (*both alike*)
With 2¾ mm. needles and MS, cast on 106 (110, 114, 118) sts. Work in k. 2, p. 2 rib until work measures 8 cm. Inc. across last row thus:
Inc. row: Rib 8 (5, 6, 9), * inc. in next st., rib 10 (10, 9, 8); rep. from * ending inc. in next st., rib 9 (5, 7, 9) – 115 (120, 125, 130) sts.
Change to 3 mm. needles and work in st. st. (*see page 13*) until work measures 36 (37, 37, 38) cm. from beg., ending with a p. row.

To shape raglan Cast off 3 sts. at beg. of next 2 rows, then dec. 1 st. at each end of every alt. row until 95 (100, 105, 110) sts. remain, thus ending with a p. row. Leave these sts. on a spare needle.

Sleeves
With 2¾ mm. needles and MS, cast on 82 (82, 90, 90) sts. Work in k. 2, p. 2 rib until work measures 5 cm.
Change to 3 mm. needles and work in st. st. inc. 1 st. at each end of every foll. sixth row until there are 90 (90, 100, 100) sts. Work straight until sleeve measures 17 (18, 18, 19) cm. from beg., ending with a p. row.

To shape raglan Cast off 3 sts. at beg. of next 2 rows, then dec. 1 st. at each end of every alt. row until 70 (70, 80, 80) sts. remain. Leave these sts. on a spare needle.

Yoke
Transfer all sts. to circular needle – 330 (340, 370, 380) sts.
Mark the beg. of yoke with a coloured thread to denote beg. of every round, and when changing yarn also mark beg. of round. Now beg. at right side of Back and work in Fair Isle pattern from charts 1, 2 and 3, across Back, first sleeve, Front, then second sleeve, and work dec. rounds as shown on charts as follows:
On seventeenth round of pink band, work * sl. 1, k. 1, p.s.s.o., k. 6, k. 2 tog.; rep. from * all round – 264 (272, 296, 304) sts.
On seventeenth round of beige band, work * sl. 1, k. 1, p.s.s.o., k. 4, k. 2 tog.; rep. from * all round – 198 (204, 222, 228) sts.
On seventh round of rust band, work *

sl. 1, k. 1, p.s.s.o., k. 2, k. 2 tog.; rep. from * all round – 132 (136, 148, 152) sts.
Now work 3 (3, 6, 6) rounds in rust, then work in k. 2, p. 2 rib for 8 rounds. Cast off ribwise.

TO MAKE UP

Fasten off all loose ends. Press work on wrong side (except rib) with a warm iron over a damp cloth. Join small raglan seams. Join sleeve and side seams. Press seams.

Work 3(366) rounds in rust
Repeat of 8 Sts.

Dec. round

Chart 3

X – rust
□ – main

Repeat of 8 Sts.

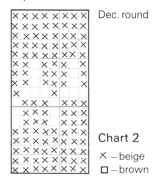

Dec. round

Chart 2

X – beige
□ – brown

Repeat of 10 Sts.

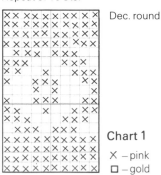

Dec. round

Chart 1

X – pink
□ – gold

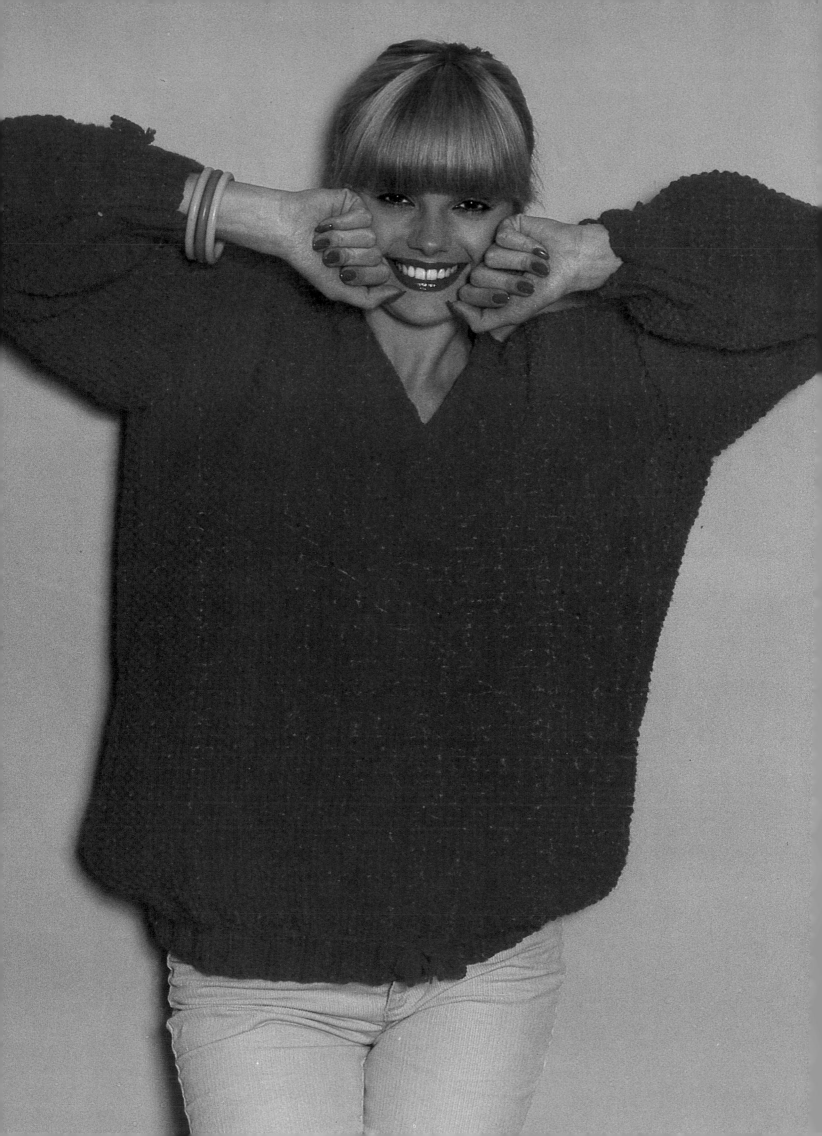

Beginner's Luck

MATERIALS

18 50 g. balls Patons Clansman D.K.; a pair each 6½ mm. (no. 3) and 5½ mm. (no. 5) knitting needles.

TENSION

7 stitches to 5 cm. over moss stitch.

MEASUREMENTS

To fit bust 34-38 in., 86-97 cm.
Length 27 in., 69 cm.
Sleeve 16½ in., 42 cm.

ABBREVIATIONS

k., knit; p., purl; st(s)., stitch(es); beg., beginning; cont., continue; dec., decreas(e)(ing); foll., following; m. 1, make one; m. st., moss stitch; rem., remaining; rep., repeat; tog., together.

NOTE

Yarn is used double throughout.

INSTRUCTIONS

Back

With 5½ mm. needles, cast on 62 sts. Work 12 rows in k. 2, p. 2 rib, beg. second row p. 2.
Change to 6½ mm. needles.
Next row: K. 1, (p. 1, k. 1, p. 1, pick up loop lying between needles and k. it – referred to as m. 1) to last 4 sts., (p. 1, k. 1) twice – 81 sts.
M. st. row: K. 1, (p. 1, k. 1) to end (see also page 13). Rep. m. st. row until work measures 53 cm. from beg.

To shape armhole Cast off 6 sts. at beg. of next 2 rows. Cont. straight until work measures 69 cm. from beg. Cast off.

Front

As Back until work measures 42 cm.

To shape neck *Next row:* M. st. 38, k. 2 tog., turn. Cont. on these sts. only. Dec. 1 st. at beg. of third row and at the same edge on every foll. third row until work measures 53 cm. from beg., ending at outer edge.

To shape armhole Still dec. at neck edge on every third row until 25 sts. remain, at the same time cast off 6 sts. at beg. of next row. Cont. straight until work measures 69 cm., ending at armhole edge. Cast off. Rejoin yarns to inner end of rem. sts., cast off centre st., k. 2 tog., m. st. to end. Complete as first side, reversing shapings.

Sleeves

With 5½ mm. needles, cast on 30 sts. Rib 14 rows as Back. Change to 6½ mm. needles.
Next row: K. 1, (m. 1, k. 1, p. 1, m. 1, p. 1, k. 1) to last st., m. 1., k. 1 – 45 sts.
Cont. in m. st. until work measures 46 cm. Cast off.

Neckband

With 5½ mm. needles, cast on 98 sts. Beg. with row 2, rib 8 rows as Back. With right side facing, cast off knitwise.

TO MAKE UP

Press work. Join shoulders. Sew cast-off edge of sleeves to armholes, placing 4 cm. of sides to cast-off groups at underarms. Join side and sleeve seams. Lapping right side over left at centre front, sew cast-on edge of neckband to neck edge, then sew down short side edges. Make a 120 cm. long twisted cord to thread through holes above rib at lower edge, then with two 50 cm. cords, finish cuffs in the same way.

White Lady

MATERIALS

11 25 g. balls Hayfield Encore; a pair each 3¾ mm. (no. 9) and 4½ mm. (no. 7) knitting needles; three small buttons.

TENSION

20 stitches and 27 rows to 10 cm. square over stocking stitch, using 4½ mm. needles.

MEASUREMENTS

To fit bust 32-34 in., 81-84 cm. (actual size 34 in., 87 cm.)
Length 21 in., 53 cm.
Sleeve seam 7 in., 18 cm.

ABBREVIATIONS

k., knit; p., purl; st(s)., stitch(es); alt., alternate; beg., beginning; cont., continue; dec., decreas(e)(ing); foll., following; inc., increas(e)(ing); inc. 1 k., increase by picking up loop between sts. and knitting into back of it; patt., pattern; p.s.s.o., pass slip stitch over; rem., remaining; rep., repeat; sl., slip; st. st., stocking stitch; tog., together; y.f., yarn forward.

INSTRUCTIONS

Back
With 3¾ mm. needles, cast on 90 sts.
Work 9 cm. in k. 2, p. 2 rib, beg. alt. rows p. 2 and dec. 1 st. at end of last row – 89 sts.
Change to 4½ mm. needles and cont. in st. st. (see page 13) until work measures 34 cm., ending after a p. row.

To shape armholes Cast off 6 sts. at beg. of next 2 rows, and 3 sts. at beg. of next 2 rows. Dec. 1 st. at both ends of next row and foll. alt. row – 67 sts.
Work 4 rows straight. K. 1 row. Cont. in patt. thus:
Row 1: K. 2, (inc. 1 k., k. 4, sl. 1, k. 2 tog., p.s.s.o., k. 4, inc. 1 k., k. 2) to end.

Fluffy white sweater with short sleeves and slightly square neck has a chevron pattern on the yoke and sleeves, and picot neck edging.

Row 2: P.
Rows 3 to 8: Rep. rows 1 and 2 three times.
Rows 9 and 10: K.
These 10 rows form the patt. *. Rep. them twice more, then rep. rows 1 and 2.

To shape neck Next row: Patt. 22, turn; leave rem. sts. on a spare needle. Dec. 1 st. at neck edge on next 6 rows – 16 sts. Work 1 row straight. Cast off. With right side facing, sl. centre 23 sts. onto spare needle, join yarn to rem. sts. and work this side of neck to match first side, reversing shapings.

Front
As Back to *. Rep. last 10 rows once more.

To shape neck Next row: Patt. 20, k. 2 tog., turn; leave rem. sts. on spare needle. Dec. 1 st. at neck edge on foll. 5 alt. rows – 16 sts. Work 9 rows straight. Cast off.
With right side facing, sl. centre 23 sts. onto a spare needle, join yarn to rem. sts., k. 2 tog., patt. to end. Complete to match first side, reversing shapings.

Sleeves
With 3¾ mm. needles, cast on 74 sts. Work 5 cm. in rib as Back, inc. 6 sts. evenly on last row – 80 sts.
Change to 4½ mm. needles. Beg. with ninth row, cont. in patt. as Back until 34 rows have been worked. Sleeve should measure approx. 18 cm.

To shape top Cast off 6 sts. at beg. of next 2 rows, and 3 sts. at beg. of next 2 rows. Dec. 1 st. at both ends of next row and foll. alt. rows until 32 sts. remain. Work 1 row. Cast off 4 sts. at beg. of next

---

2 rows. Cast off, working 2 tog. all across row.

Neck edging
Join right shoulder seam. With right side facing and using 3¾ mm. needles, pick up and k. 17 sts. down left front neck, k. 2 tog., k. 19, k. 2 tog. across centre front sts., pick up and k. 17 sts. up right front neck, 9 sts. down right back neck, k. 2 tog., k. 19, k. 2 tog. across centre back sts., pick up and k. 9 sts. up left back neck – 94 sts. Beg. p. row, work 3 rows in st. st.
Next row (hemline): K. 2, (y.f., k. 2 tog.) to end. Beg. p. row, work 3 rows in st. st. Cast off.

TO MAKE UP

Do not press. Join left shoulder seam for 2 cm. Join side and sleeve seams. Sew in sleeves. Fold neck edging at hemline to wrong side and slip-stitch. Sew buttons to left back shoulder and make button-loops on front shoulder to correspond.

New Yorker

Ultra-slim and sophisticated jacket knitted in stocking stitch, with set-in pockets and a garter stitch shawl collar.
Very easy

MATERIALS

10 (11, 12) 50 g. balls Patons Clansman D.K.; a pair each 3¾ mm. (no. 9) and 4 mm. (no. 8) knitting needles; one button; two shoulder pads.

TENSION

22 stitches and 30 rows to 10 cm. square.

MEASUREMENTS

To fit bust 32 (34, 36) in., 81 (86, 91) cm.
Length 22½ (22½, 23) in., 57 (57, 58) cm.
Sleeve seam (all sizes) 16½ in., 42 cm.

ABBREVIATIONS

k., knit; p., purl; st(s)., stitch(es); alt., alternate; beg., beginning; cont., continue; dec. decreas(e)(ing); foll., following; g-st., garter stitch; inc., increas(e)-(ing); patt., pattern; rem., remaining; rep., repeat; sl., slip; st. st., stocking stitch.

INSTRUCTIONS

Back

With 3¾ mm. needles, cast on 98 (103, 109) sts. Work 6 rows in g-st. (see page 13).
Change to 4 mm. needles and cont. in st. st. (see page 13) until work measures 37 cm.

To shape armholes Cast off 4 sts. at beg. of next 2 rows and 3 sts. at beg. of foll. 2 rows. Dec. 1 st. at both ends of next row and foll. alt. row – 80 (85, 91) sts.
Cont. straight until armholes measure 20 (20, 21) cm.

To shape shoulders Cast off 7 (7, 8) sts. at beg. of next 6 rows and 5 (7, 7) sts. at beg. of foll. 2 rows. Cast off rem. 28 (29, 29) sts.

Right front

With 3¾ mm. needles, cast on 66 (69, 72) sts. Work 6 rows in g-st.
Change to 4 mm. needles and cont. thus:
Row 1: K.
Row 2: P. to last 7 sts., k. to end. Rep. the last 2 rows until work measures 24 cm., ending with a wrong side row.
Buttonhole row: K. 3, cast off 2, k. to end.
Next row: P. to last 5 sts., k. 2, cast on 2, k. to end.
Rep. rows 1 and 2 until work measures 26 cm., ending at side edge.

To shape neck Work to last 7 sts., turn; sl. these 7 sts. onto a safety-pin. Dec. 1 st. at neck edge on next row and every foll. third row until work measures 37 cm., ending at side edge.

To shape armhole Still dec. at neck edge as before, cast off 4 sts. at beg. of next row and 3 sts. at beg. of foll. alt. row; then dec. 1 st. at armhole edge on foll. 2 alt. rows. Keeping armhole edge straight, cont. dec. at neck as before until 26 (28, 31) sts. remain. Cont. straight until Front matches Back to shoulder, ending at armhole.

To shape shoulder Cast off 7 (7, 8) sts. at beg. of next row and foll. 2 alt. rows. Work 1 row and cast off.

Left front

Omitting buttonhole, work as Right Front, reversing shapings and position of g-st. border.

Sleeves

With 3¾ mm. needles, cast on 50 (50, 54) sts. Work 6 rows in g-st.
Change to 4 mm. needles. Work in st. st., inc. 1 st. at both ends of seventh row and every foll. eighth row until there are 74 (74, 78) sts. Cont. straight until work measures 42 cm., ending with a p. row.

To shape top Cast off 4 sts. at beg. of next 2 rows. Dec. 1 st. at both ends of next row and every foll. alt. row until 24 sts. remain. Work 1 row. Cast off 3 sts. at beg. of next 4 rows. Cast off.

Collar

Join shoulder seams. With 4 mm. needles and wrong side facing, join yarn to 7 sts. on safety-pin at Right Front, k. to end. Cont. in g-st., inc. 1 st. at end of next row and every foll. fourth row until there are 24 sts. Cont. straight until work, when slightly stretched, will fit up shaped edge of Front to shoulder, ending straight (outside) edge. Cont. thus:
Row 1: K. 20, turn.
Row 2: Sl. 1, k. to end.
Rows 3 and 4: K. to end. Rep. rows 1 to 4 three times more. Cont. straight on all sts. until work reaches centre back neck. Cast off.
With 4 mm. needles and right side facing, join yarn to 7 sts. on safety-pin at Left Front and work to match first side.

Pockets (*two*)

With 4 mm. needles, cast on 28 sts. Beg. k. row, work 11 cm. in st. st., then 6 rows in g-st. Cast off.

TO MAKE UP

Press, following instructions on the ball band. Join side and sleeve seams. Sew in sleeves. Sew on collar, joining short ends at centre back neck. Sew on pockets and buttons. Sew in shoulder pads.

Sugar

Subtle mohair Fair Isle sweater with a V-neck. One simple Fair Isle motif is repeated through the sweater in different shades, and texture is added by working French knots here and there on the Fair Isle.
Easy Fair Isle

MATERIALS

Sweater 7 (8) balls Pingouin Mohair in main shade – rose (no. 325), 3 (3) balls in first contrast shade – white (no. 301), 2 (2) balls in second contrast shade – perle (no. 326) and 1 (1) ball in third contrast shade – cosmos (no. 335); a pair each 5 mm. (no. 6) and 5½ mm. (no. 5) knitting needles; a darning needle.
Socks 5 balls Pingouin Mohair in main shade – rose (no. 325) and 1 ball in each of three contrast shades – white (no. 301), perle (no. 326) and cosmos (no. 335); a set of four 5 mm. (no. 6) knitting needles.

TENSION

Sweater 17 stitches and 19 rows to 10 cm.
Socks 15 stitches and 17 rows to 10 cm.

MEASUREMENTS

Sweater To fit bust 32-34 (36-38) in., 81-86 (91-96) cm.
Length to centre back 28¼ (28¾) in., 72 (73) cm.
Sleeve (both sizes) 18 in., 43 cm.
Socks To fit 4½-5½ shoe size.
Length to top of heel without top folded over 17¾ in., 45 cm.

ABBREVIATIONS

k., knit; p., purl; st(s)., stitch(es); alt., alternate; beg., beginning; cont., continue; dec(s)., decrease(s); foll., following; inc(s)., increase(s); patt., pattern; p.s.s.o., pass slip stitch over; rem., remaining; rep., repeat; sep., separately; sl., slip; st. st., stocking stitch; tog., together; A., main shade (rose); B., first contrast (white); C., second contrast (perle – grey); D., third contrast (cosmos – lilac).

INSTRUCTIONS

Sweater

Back
With 5 mm. needles and A., cast on 78 (86) sts. Work in k. 2, p. 2 rib for 7 cm., ending with a right side row.
Inc. row: Work 4 incs. evenly along next rib row – 82 (90) sts.
Change to 5½ mm. needles and work 4 rows in st. st. (see page 13).
Now work Fair Isle from chart, using B. and D. as contrast shades as shown, working rows 1 to 16 once. Rep. these 16 rows once again, but using B. and C. as contrast shades.
These 32 rows form patt. **. When the 32 rows have been completed twice, rep. rows 1 to 16 once more.

To shape armholes Cast off 5 sts. at beg. of next 2 rows and 2 sts. at beg. of foll. 2 rows. Now dec. 1 st. at each end of every alt. row until 60 (68) sts. remain. Cont. in patt. until work measures 20 (21) cm. from beg. of armhole shaping.

To shape shoulders Cast off 5 (6) sts. at beg. of next 4 rows and 6 (8) sts. at beg. of next 2 rows. Leave rem. 28 sts. on a spare needle, to be worked later as neckband.

Front
Exactly as Back to **. Rep. the 32 rows of patt. once, then rows 1 to 12 once more.

To shape V-neck Work 40 (44), place centre 2 sts. on a safety-pin. Finish each side sep. Dec. 1 st. at neck edge on next and every foll. third row until 16 (20) sts. remain. Meanwhile, when row 16 of third patt. rep. has been completed, shape armhole as set for Back. Cont. to shape neck as set to 16 (20) sts. then work straight until length matches that of Back to beg. of shoulder shaping.

To shape shoulder Beg. at outside edge, cast off 5 (6) sts. at beg. of next 2 rows, then cast off rem. sts.
Rejoin yarn and complete other side of neck to match.

Sleeves

With 5 mm. needles and A., cast on 46 (54) sts. Work in k. 2, p. 2 rib for 7 cm., ending with a right side row.
Inc. row: Work 12 incs. evenly along next rib row – 58 (66) sts.
Change to 5½ mm. needles and work 4 rows in st. st. Now work Fair Isle from chart, working rows 17 to 32 once; then working rows 1 to 32 once, and then rows 1 to 16 once more.

To shape armholes Cast off 5 sts. at beg. of next 2 rows, and 2 sts. at beg. of foll. 2 rows – 44 (52) sts.
Now dec. 1 st. at each end of every alt. row until 20 (24) sts. remain. Cast off 3 sts. at beg. of next 4 rows. Cast off rem. sts.
Join right shoulder seam.

Neckband

With 5 mm. needles and right side facing and with A., pick up and k. 36 (38) sts. along left neck edge. K. the 2 sts. at centre neck, then pick up and k. 36 (38) sts. along right neck edge and k. across the 28 sts. of back neck – 102 (106) sts.
Work in k. 2, p. 2 rib, but dec. 1 st. at either side of the 2 centre sts. on every row until 7 rib rows have been completed. Work 1 row straight. Now work 7 more rows in k. 2, p. 2 rib, but inc. 1 st. at either side of the 2 centre sts. on every row. Cast off loosely ribwise.

TO MAKE UP

Join neckband seam on the inside and join left shoulder seam. Fold neckband in half and stitch down on the inside. Set in sleeves. Join sleeve seams. Join side seams, matching up patt.

French knots

With each of the contrast shades B., C. and D., using yarn double, work French

KEY
Pingouin Mohair

□ main shade 325
V white 301
● cosmos 335
X perle 326
■ white 301

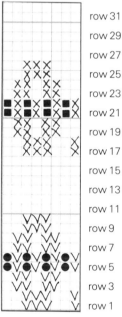

row 31
row 29
row 27
row 25
row 23
row 21
row 19
row 17
row 15
row 13
row 11
row 9
row 7
row 5
row 3
row 1

8 pattern stitches plus one selvedge stitch at each end of every row

knots with the darning needle, randomly in the centre of some of the Fair Isle motifs (as shown in the photograph).

Socks

With a set of four 5 mm. needles and A., cast on 56 sts. Arrange these sts. on three of the four needles with 18 sts. on two needles and 20 sts. on the third. Work 10 rows in k. 2, p. 2 rib (mark end of round). Work 4 rounds in st. st. (see page 13). Now work the 32 rows of Fair Isle patt. once, then rows 1 to 16 once more. Now work straight in st. st. and A. until work measures 35 cm. from beg.

To shape leg *Next row:* K. 1, sl. 1, k. 1, p.s.s.o., k. to last 3 sts., k. 2 tog., k. 1. Work 4 rounds without shaping; rep. last 5 rounds until 42 sts. remain.

To divide for heel With A., work as follows:
Next row: Sl. first and last 11 sts. of round onto one needle, rejoin yarn and p. to end – 22 sts.
Beg. with a k. row, work 16 rows in st. st., ending with a p. row.

To turn heel *Next row:* K. 14, sl. 1, k. 1, p.s.s.o., turn;
Next row: P. 7, p. 2 tog., turn;
Next row: K. 7, sl. 1, k. 1, p.s.s.o., turn;
Next row: P. 7, p. 2 tog., turn;
Rep. last 2 rows until all sts. are on one needle.
Next round: K. 4, using second needle, k. rem. 4 heel sts., k. up 10 sts. down side of heel using third needle, k. across 20 sts. of instep using fourth needle, k. up 10 sts. up other side of heel, then k. the first 4 sts. onto this needle.

To shape instep *Round 1:* K. to end.
Round 2: First needle: K. to last 3 sts., k. 2 tog., k. 1; second needle: k. to end; third needle: k. 1, sl. 1, p.s.s.o., k. to end. Rep. rounds 1 and 2 until 42 sts. remain. Cont. without shaping until work measures 14 cm. from where sts. were picked up at heel.

To shape toe *Round 1:* First needle: K. to last 3 sts., k. 2 tog., k. 1; second needle: k. 1, sl. 1, k. 1., p.s.s.o., k. to last 3 sts., k. 2 tog., k. 1; third needle: k. 1, sl. 1, k. 1, p.s.s.o., k. to end.
Work 2 rounds in st. st. without shaping. Rep. last 3 rounds until 24 sts. remain, then k. across sts. on first needle. Cast off, knitting the 2 rows tog. on the wrong side, or graft sts. tog.
Embroider with French knots as on the sweater.

Coco

Classic Chanel-style suit in a marvellous mixture of yarns: cerise, steel grey and black with a speck of glitter.

MATERIALS

6 (6, 7, 7) 50 g. balls Pingouin Laine et Mohair in Fuschia; 6 (6, 7, 7) 50 g. balls Pingouin Confort in Souris; 1 50 g. ball Pingouin Confort in Noir; 4 (4, 5, 5) 50 g. balls Pingouin Granitée in Guinée; a pair 4 mm. (no. 8) and a pair 3¾ mm. (no. 9) double pointed knitting needles; a stitch-holder; two shoulder pads; waist-length elastic.

TENSION

12 stitches and 23 rows to 5 cm.

MEASUREMENTS

To fit bust 32 (34, 36, 38) in., 81 (86, 91, 97) cm.
Hips 34 (36, 38, 40) in., 86 (91, 97, 102) cm.
Jacket length 21¼ (21¾, 22¼, 22¾) in., 54 (55, 56, 57) cm.
Sleeve (all sizes) 17¾ in., 45 cm.
Skirt length (all sizes) 25½ in., 65 cm.

ABBREVIATIONS

k., knit; p., purl; st(s)., stitch(es); alt., alternate; beg., beginning; cont., continue; dec., decreas(e)(ing); foll., following; g-st., garter stitch; inc., increas(e)(ing), patt., pattern; rep., repeat; sl., slip; st. st., stocking stitch; tog., together; y.bk., yarn back; y.fd., yarn forward; A, Fuschia; B, Souris; C, Guinée; D, Noir.

INSTRUCTIONS

Jacket

Back
With 4 mm. needles and B, cast on 122 (130, 134, 142) sts.
Cont. with B and patt. thus:
Row 1 (right side): K. 1, (k. 3, with yarn at back sl. 1 purlwise) to last st., k. 1.
Row 2: K. 1, (y.fd. between needles, sl. 1 purlwise, y.bk. between needles, k. 3) to last st., k. 1.
Change to A.
Row 3: K. 1, (k. 1, with yarn at back sl. 1 purlwise, k. 2) to last st., k. 1.
Row 4: K. 1, (k. 2, y.fd. between needles, sl. 1 purlwise, y.bk. between needles, k. 1) to last st., k. 1.
Change to C.
Rows 5 and 6: As rows 1 and 2.
Change to B.
Rows 7 and 8: As rows 3 and 4.
Change to A.
Rows 9 and 10: As rows 1 and 2.
Change to C.
Rows 11 and 12: As rows 3 and 4.
These 12 rows form stripe patt. Patt. until work measures 35 cm.

To shape armhole Cast off 5 (5, 6, 6) sts. at beg. of next 2 rows. Dec. 1 st. at beg. of every row until 98 (102, 102, 106) sts. remain. Cont. straight until work measures 53 (54, 55, 56) cm. Cast off.

Pocket linings (*two*)
With 3¾ mm. needles and B, cast on 24 sts.
Beg. k., work 11 cm. in st. st. (see page 13), ending with a p. row. Leave these sts. on a stitch-holder.

Left front
With 4 mm. needles and B, cast on 62 (66, 70, 74) sts.
Patt. as Back until work measures 13 cm from beg., ending with a complete C stripe.
Pocket opening row: Patt. 23 (25, 27, 29), cast off 24 sts., with right side facing, patt. 24 sts. of one pocket lining, patt. 15 (17, 19, 21) sts.
Patt. straight until work measures 35 cm. from beg., ending with a wrong side row.

To shape armhole Cast off 5 (5, 6, 6) sts. at beg. of next row. Dec. 1 st. at beg. of every foll. alt. row until 50 (52, 54, 56) sts. remain. Cont. straight until work measures 46 (46, 47, 47) cm., ending with a right side row.

To shape neck Cast off 9 (10, 10, 11) sts. at beg. of next row. Dec. 1 st. at beg. of every foll. alt. row until 32 (33, 35, 36) sts. remain. Cont. straight until work measures 53 (54, 55, 56) cm. Cast off.

Right front
As Left Front, reversing pocket opening row and shapings.

Sleeves
With 4 mm. needles and B, cast on 62 (66, 70, 74) sts.
Patt. as Back, inc. 1 st. at each end of every twentieth row until there are 82

(86, 90, 94) sts. Cont. straight until work measures 44 cm. from beg.

To shape top Cast off 5 (5, 6, 6) sts. at beg. of next 2 rows. Dec. 1 st. at beg. of every row until 22 sts. remain. Cast off 3 sts. at beg. of next 4 rows. Cast off.

Skirt

Back and front (*both alike*)
With 4 mm. needles and C, cast on 118 (122, 130, 134) sts.
Patt. as Back of jacket until work measures 22 cm., ending with a wrong side row.
Dec. 1 st. at each end of next and every foll. sixteenth row until 106 (110, 118, 122) sts. remain, then dec. 1 st. at each end of every foll. sixth row until 84 (88, 96, 100) sts. remain. Cont. straight until work measures 62 cm. from beg., ending with a wrong side row.
Change to D. For waistband, work 3 cm. in g-st. (see page 13). Cast off loosely.

TO MAKE UP

Do not press.
Jacket: Join shoulder seams. Set in sleeves. Join side and sleeve seams. Sew down pocket linings on wrong side.
Edging: With 3¾ mm. needles and D, cast on 5 sts.
Cont. thus: * K. 5, do not turn work, but return needle to left hand, slipping sts. back along needle to point, draw yarn tight behind sts.; rep. from * until tube is long enough when slightly stretched to fit round entire outer edge. Cast off. Join ends and placing this seam to centre of cast-on edge of Back, sew tube over 1 st. of edge of jacket. Finish sleeve edges and pocket tops in the same way. Sew in shoulder pads.
Skirt: Join sides. Join elastic in a ring and herringbone to wrong side of waistband.

Tender Touch

See photograph on following pages.

MATERIALS

8 (9) 40 g. balls Pingouin Mohair in main shade (flamant rose) and 3 (3) balls in contrast shade (sable); a pair each 5 mm. (no. 6) and 6 mm. (no. 4) knitting needles.

TENSION

14 stitches and 18 rows to 10 cm. over stocking stitch.

MEASUREMENTS

To fit bust 32-34 (36-38) in., 82-87 (92-97) cm.
Length 34 (34½) in., 86 (87) cm.

ABBREVIATIONS

k., knit; p., purl; st(s)., stitch(es); alt., alternate; beg., beginning; cont., continue; dec., decrease; foll., following; inc(s)., increase(s); mb., knit into the front and back of next st. 4 times, yarn over needle, lift the 4 sts. over the yarn over needle; patt., pattern; rep., repeat; st. st., stocking stitch; y.o.n., yarn over needle; MS, main shade (flamant rose); CS, contrast shade (sable).

INSTRUCTIONS

Back
With 5 mm. needles and MS, cast on 69 (75) sts. Work in k. 1, p. 1 rib for 8 cm. Change to 6 mm. needles and work the foll. patt.:
Rows 1 to 6: Beg. with a k. row, work 6 rows in st. st. (see page 13).
Row 7: (P. 3, k. 3) to last 3 sts., p. 3.
Row 8: As row 7 (p. the k. sts. and k. the p. sts. as they face you.)
Work these 8 rows once more.
Rows 17 to 20: Beg. with a k. row., work 4 rows in st. st.
Row 21: (K. 3, p. 1, mb., p. 1) to last 3 sts., k. 3.

Row 22: P.
Rows 23 to 25: Beg. with a k. row, work 3 rows in st. st.
Row 26: Change to CS and p. one row.
Rep. rows 7 to 25.
Change to MS and p. one row.
Rep. rows 7 to 25.
Change to CS and p. one row.
Rep. rows 7 to 24.

To shape raglans Cast off 2 sts., k. to end.
Next row: Change to MS, cast off 2 sts., and p. to end – 65 (71) sts.
Working in MS from now on, rep. rows 7 to 26 but dec. 1 st. at each end of next and every foll. alt. row, keeping patt. sequence, until 33 sts. remain. Do not cast off.

Front
Exactly as Back.

Sleeves
With 5 mm. needles and MS, cast on 42 (46) sts. Work in k. 1, p. 1 rib for 8 cm., ending with a right side row.
Inc. row: Work 9 (11) incs. evenly along this rib row – 51 (57) sts.
Change to 6 mm. needles and work rows 9 to 26 of the patt. as set for Back once only. Rep. rows 7 to 26 once, then rep. rows 7 to 25. Change to CS and work row 26. Rep. rows 7 to 24.

To shape raglans Cast off 2 sts., k. to end.
Next row: Change to MS, cast off 2 sts., and p. to end – 47 (53) sts.
Cont. to work in MS and work patt. to match Back, but dec. 1 st. at each end of next and every foll. alt. row until 15 sts. remain. Do not cast off.

Neckband
With right side facing and MS and 5 mm.

needles, work in k. 1, p. 1 rib along the 15 sts. of left sleeve, the 33 sts. of front, the 15 sts. of right sleeve and the 33 sts. of back. Work 18 rows in k. 1, p. 1 rib then cast off ribwise.

TO MAKE UP

Join raglan seams. Join side seams (see below). Join neckband and fold it in half and stitch down on the inside.

Side split edgings
When joining side seams, begin at top of first contrast stripe and join remainder of seam up to armhole.
Edge side splits as follows:
With 5 mm. needles and MS, cast on 8 sts. and work in k. 1, p. 1 rib for the length from the bottom edge to the beg. of first contrast stripe. Change to CS and cont. in rib for length of first contrast stripe. Cast off. Work 3 more strips in the same way.
Stitch these strips to each edge of side splits, sewing down top edges.

Extra-long mohair sweater in delicate shades of pink and beige has a subtle all-over pattern, loose round neck, and splits at the sides.

Belle du Jour

MATERIALS

9 100 g. balls Twilleys Pegasus (grey – shade no. 15); a pair each 3¼ mm. (no. 11) and 4 mm. (no. 8) knitting needles; five buttons.

TENSION

23 stitches and 24 rows to 10 cm. (4 in.) over pattern.

MEASUREMENTS

One size only: to fit bust 34-38 in., 86-97 cm.
Length: 23½ in., 60 cm.
Sleeve seam: 15½ in., 39 cm.

ABBREVIATIONS

k., knit; p., purl; st(s)., stitch(es); alt., alternate; beg., beginning; cont., continue; dec., decreas(e)(ing); foll., following; inc(s)., increase(s); patt(s)., pattern(s); rem., remaining; rep(s)., repeat(s); st. st., stocking stitch; t.b.l., through back of loop; tog., together; y.f., yarn forward; y.o.n., yarn over needle.

INSTRUCTIONS

Back

With 3¼ mm. needles, cast on 98 sts.
Work 16 rows in k. 1, p. 1 rib.
Inc. row: Work 10 incs. evenly along row – 108 sts.
Change to 4 mm. needles and patt. thus:
Row 1: K.
Row 2: P.
Row 3: * (K. 2 tog.) three times, (y.o.n., k. 1) six times, (k. 2 tog.) three times *; rep. from * to * to end.
Row 4: K.
These 4 rows form patt. Rep. patt. 21 times in all, keeping patt. correct.

To shape armholes Cast off 7 sts. at beg. of next 2 rows.
Next row: Cast off 5 sts., k. 6 (including the st. already on the needle), work in

Baggy cotton cardigan in feather and fan stitch has knitted lace strips which emphasise shoulder seams.

patt. to last 11 sts., k. 11.
Next row: Cast off 5 sts., k. to end.
Dec. 1 st. at each end of the next 2 rows – 80 sts.
(Work the 4 sts. at each end of every row as k. on rows 1, 3 and 4 of patt. and as p. on row 2.)
Work the rest of the row in patt. until 12 patts. have been worked from beg. of armhole shaping. Working in st. st. (see page 13) from now on, work 4 rows.

To shape neck K. 27, k. 2 tog., turn; at neck edge dec. 1 st. on every row until 23 sts. remain. Cast off. Cast off centre 22 sts., then complete to match other side of neck.

Right front

With 3¼ mm. needles, cast on 48 sts.
Work 16 rows in k. 1, p. 1 rib.
Inc. row: Inc. into every eighth st. – 54 sts.
Change to 4 mm. needles and work patt. as set for Back until 19 patt. reps. have been worked.

To shape neck Dec. 1 st. at neck edge on first row of every patt., i.e.
1st patt. rep.: Row 1: K. 2 tog., k. to end.
Row 2: P.
Row 3: K. 1, (k. 2 tog.) twice, k. 1, (y.o.n., k. 1) five times, (k. 2 tog.) three times, work in patt. to end.
Row 4: K.
2nd patt. rep.: Working rows 1, 2 and 4 as for patt. rep. 1, work row 3 thus:
(K. 2 tog.) twice, k. 1, (y.o.n., k. 1) five times, (k. 2 tog.) three times, work in patt. to end – 52 sts.
When these 2 patts. have been completed, shape right armhole as Back and at the same time dec. at neck edge thus:
Work rows 1, 2 and 4 as for patt. rep. 1 for every patt., but work row 3 as follows:
3rd patt. rep.: Row 3: K. 1, k. 2 tog., k. 2,

(y.o.n., k. 1) four times, (k. 2 tog.) three times, work in patt. to end – 38 sts.
4th patt. rep.: Row 3: K. 2 tog., k. 2, (y.o.n., k. 1) four times, (k. 2 tog.) three times, work in patt. to end – 36 sts.
5th patt. rep.: Row 3: K. 4, (y.o.n., k. 1) three times, (k. 2 tog.) three times, work in patt. to end – 35 sts.
6th patt. rep.: Row 3: K. 3, (y.o.n., k. 1) three times, (k. 2 tog.) three times, work in patt. to end – 34 sts.
7th patt. rep.: Row 3: K. 2, (y.o.n., k. 1) three times, (k. 2 tog.) three times, work in patt. to end – 33 sts.
8th patt. rep.: Row 3: K. 1, (y.o.n., k. 1) three times, (k. 2 tog.) three times, work in patt. to end – 32 sts.
9th patt. rep.: Row 3: (Y.o.n., k. 1) three times, (k. 2 tog.) three times, work in patt. to end – 31 sts.
10th patt. rep.: Row 3: K. 1, (y.o.n., k. 1) twice, k. 1, (k. 2 tog.) twice, work in patt. to end – 30 sts.
11th patt. rep.: Row 3: (Y.o.n., k. 1) twice, k. 1, (k. 2 tog.) twice, work in patt. to end – 29 sts.
12th patt. rep.: Row 3: (Y.o.n., k. 1) twice, (k. 2 tog.) twice, work in patt. to end – 28 sts.
13th patt. rep.: Row 3: Y.o.n., k. 3, k. 2 tog., work in patt. to end – 27 sts.
14th patt. rep.: Row 3: Y.o.n., k. 2, k. 2 tog., work in patt. to end – 26 sts.
Now work in st. st. and work a dec. on the foll. alt. row and the 2 foll. fourth rows – 23 sts.
When length matches that of Back, cast off.

Left front

As Right Front, reversing all shapings.

Sleeves

With 3¼ mm. needles, cast on 52 sts.
Work 16 rows in k. 1, p. 1 rib.
Inc. row: Rib 7, inc. into next and every alt. st. to last 6 sts., rib 6 – 72 sts.
Change to 4 mm. needles and work in patt. as for Back eight times in all.
Now inc. 1 st. at each end of next and every foll. twelfth row until there are 80 sts., working these extra sts. as k. on rows 1, 3 and 4 and as p. on row 2.
Cont. until work measures 39 cm. from beg.

To shape top Instead of working patt., work rows 1, 3 and 4 as k. and row 2 as p.

Cast off 7 sts. at beg. of next 2 rows and 3 sts. at beg. of foll. 2 rows. Now dec. 1 st. at each end of every alt. row until 26 sts. remain. Cast off 6 sts. at beg. of next 2 rows. Cast off rem. sts.

Shoulder trimmings (*two*)

With 4 mm. needles, cast on 112 sts. Patt. thus:

Row 1: K. 1, y.f. and over to make 1, * k. 5, lift second, third, fourth and fifth sts. over first and off needle, y.f. *; rep. from * to * to last st., k. 1.

Row 2: K. 1, * (p. 1, y.o.n. to make 1, k. 1 t.b.l.) all into next st., p. 1 *; rep. from * to * to end. Cast off.

Front band

Join shoulder seams, pressing seam flat. With 3¼ mm. needles and right side facing and beg. at right bottom edge, pick up and k. 72 sts. along right front edge, 52 sts. along right neck edge, 38 sts. along back neck and 52 sts. along left neck edge, then 72 sts. down left front edge. K. 5 rows.

Buttonhole row: K. 6, * cast off 2 sts., k. 13 * (each buttonhole is spaced 14 sts. apart); rep. from * to * four times more, k. to end.

Next row: K., but cast on 2 sts. in place of cast off sts., over the 5 buttonholes.

K. 2 more rows. Cast off.

TO MAKE UP

Set in sleeves. Join side and sleeve seams. Sew on shoulder trimmings. Sew on buttons.

Lipstick

16 (17, 18) 50 g. balls Hayfield Beaulon D.K. (shade 50065); a pair each 4½ mm. (no. 7) and 5½ mm. (no. 5) knitting needles; seven buttons; a stitch-holder.

TENSION

12 stitches (2 patterns) to 6 cm.; 12 rows (1 pattern) to 5 cm.

MEASUREMENTS

To fit bust 32-34 (36-38, 40-42) in., 81-86 (91-97, 102-107) cm.
Length (all sizes) 23¾ in., 60 cm.
Sleeve (all sizes) 18 in., 46 cm.

ABBREVIATIONS

k., knit; p. purl; st(s)., stitch(es); beg., beginning; dec., decrease; inc., increase; patt., pattern; rep., repeat; st. st., stocking stitch; tog., together.

INSTRUCTIONS

Back
With 4½ mm. needles, cast on 78 (86, 94) sts. Work 10 cm. in k. 2, p. 2 rib, beg. second row p. 2.
Inc. row: Rib 5 (3, 1), (inc. in next st., rib 2) to last 4 (2, 0) sts., rib 4 (2, 0) – 101 (113, 125) sts.
Change to 5½ mm. needles and patt. thus:
Row 1 (right side): P. 2, (k. 1, p. 2) to end.
Row 2: K. 2, (p. 1, k. 2) to end.
Row 3: P. 2, then (k. 1, p. 1) into next st. twice, * p. 2, k. 1, p. 2, then (k. 1, p. 1) into next st. twice *; rep. from * to * to last 2 sts., p. 2.
Row 4: K. 2, * p. 4, k. 2, p. 1, k. 2 *; rep. from * to * to last 6 sts., p. 4, k. 2.
Row 5: P. 6, turn; k. 4, turn; p. 6, * k. 1, p. 6, turn; k. 4, turn; p. 6 *; rep. from * to * to end.
Row 6: K. 2, * p. 4 tog., k. 2, p. 1, k. 2 *;

rep. from * to * to last 6 sts., p. 4 tog., k. 2.
Row 7: As row 1.
Row 8: As row 2.
Row 9: P. 2, * k. 1, p. 2, then (k. 1, p. 1) into next st. twice, p. 2 *; rep. from * to * to last 3 sts., k. 1, p. 2.
Row 10: K. 2, p. 1, * k. 2, p. 4, k. 2, p. 1 *; rep. from * to * to last 2 sts., k. 2.
Row 11: P. 2, * k. 1, p. 6, turn; k. 4, turn; p. 6 *; rep. from * to * to last 3 sts., k. 1, p. 2.
Row 12: K. 2, p. 1, * k. 2, p. 4 tog., k. 2, p. 1 *; rep. from * to * to last 2 sts., k. 2.
These 12 rows form patt. Patt. until work measures 60 cm., ending with a row 12 patt. row. Cast off.

Left front
With 4½ mm. needles, cast on 42 (46, 50) sts. Rib 10 cm. as Back.
Inc. row: Rib 4 (3, 2), (inc. in next st., rib 2, inc. in next st., rib 1) to last 3 sts., rib to end – 56 (62, 68) sts.
Change to 5½ mm. needles and patt. thus:
Row 1 (right side): As row 1 of Back.
Row 2: As row 2 of Back **.
Row 3: Rep. from * to * of row 3 of Back to last 2 sts., p. 2.
Row 4: K. 2; rep. from * to * of row 4 of Back to end.
Row 5: P. 2; rep. from * to * of row 5 of Back to end.
Row 6: K. 2; rep. from * to * of row 6 of Back to end.
Rows 7 and 8: As rows 1 and 2.
Row 9: As row 3 of Back, finishing p. 2, k. 1, p. 2.
Row 10: As row 10 of Back, ending last rep. k. 2.
Row 11: As row 5 of Back to last 3 sts., k. 1, p. 2.
Row 12: As row 12 of Back, ending last rep. k. 2.
These 12 rows form patt. Patt. until work

measures 60 cm., ending with a row 12 patt. row. Cast off.

Right front
As Left Front to **.
Row 3: As row 3 of Back, finishing p. 2, k. 1, p. 2.
Row 4: K. 2, p. 1, k. 2; rep. from * to * and complete as row 4 of Back.
Row 5: As row 5 of Back to last 3 sts., k. 1, p. 2.
Row 6: K. 2, p. 1, k. 2; rep. from * to * and complete as row 6 of Back.
Rows 7 and 8: As rows 1 and 2 of Back.
Row 9: P. 2; rep. from * to * of row 9 of Back to end.
Row 10: Rep. from * to * of row 10 of Back to last 2 sts., k. 2.
Row 11: P. 2; rep. from * to * of row 11 of Back to end.
Row 12: Rep. from * to * of row 12 of Back to last 2 sts., k. 2.
These 12 rows form patt. Patt. until work measures 60 cm., ending with a row 12 patt. row. Cast off.

Sleeves
With 4½ mm. needles, cast on 42 (46, 50) sts. Rib 6 cm. as Back.
Inc. row: K. 1, (inc. in next st., rib 1) nine (ten, eleven) times, (inc. in next st.) five times, (rib 1, inc. in next st.) nine (ten, eleven) times – 65 (71, 77) sts.
Change to 5½ mm. needles. Patt. as Back until work measures 46 cm. Cast off loosely.

Front bands and collar
Join shoulder seams for 36 (39, 41) sts. from each end of Back and outer edge of Fronts. * With 4½ mm. needles, cast on 12 sts.
Row 1: K. 3, (p. 2, k. 2) twice, k. 1.
Row 2: K. 1, (p. 2, k. 2) twice, p. 2, k. 1.
These 2 rows form rib *. Rep. these last 2 rows sixty-five times more. Break off yarn. Leave sts. on a stitch-holder. Rep. from * to * once more. Rep. 2 rib rows once more.
Next row (make buttonhole): Rib 5, cast off 2, rib 5.
Next row: Rib 5, cast on 2, rib 5.
Rib 20 rows, then rep. 2 buttonhole rows again. Rep. last 22 rows four times more,

thus completing sixth buttonhole. Rib 16 rows.

Next row: Rib 12, then onto same needle, pick up and k. 76 (84, 92) sts. evenly round neck, beg. at end with broken yarn rib 12 sts. of buttonband. Rib 3 rows.

Next row (make buttonhole): Rib 5, cast off 2, rib to end.

Next row: Rib to last 5 sts., cast on 2, rib 5. Rib until collar measures 8 cm. Cast off.

TO MAKE UP

Beg. and ending 16 (17.5, 19) cm. from shoulder seams, sew sleeves on sides. Join side and sleeve seams. Sew on front bands and buttons.

Shetland Lace

MATERIALS

11 (11, 12) 2 oz. hanks A.N.I. Scottish Homespun Wool; a pair each 4 mm. (no. 8), 3¼ mm. (no. 10) and 2¾ mm. (no. 12) knitting needles; seven buttons.

TENSION

14 stitches (2 patterns) to 6 cm.

MEASUREMENTS

To fit bust 34 (36, 38) in., 86 (91, 97) cm.
Length (all sizes) 24¼ in., 62 cm.
Sleeve (all sizes) 12¼ in., 31 cm.

ABBREVIATIONS

k., knit; p., purl; st(s)., stitch(es); beg., beginning; dec., decrease; inc., increase; patt(s)., pattern(s); rep., repeat; t.b.l., through back of loop; tog., together; y.fd., yarn forward; y.r.n., yarn round needle.

INSTRUCTIONS

Back
With 2¾ mm. needles, cast on 105 (117, 129) sts.
Row 1: K. 1, (p. 1, k. 2) to last 2 sts., p. 1, k. 1.
Row 2: P. 1, (k. 1, p. 2) to last 2 sts., k. 1, p. 1.
Rep. rows 1 and 2 five times more, then row 1 again **.
Inc. row: Rib 0 (2, 4), * inc. in next st., rib 4; rep. from * to end – 126 (140, 154) sts.
Change to 4 mm. needles and patt. thus:
Row 1: K. 2, (k. 2 tog., y.fd., k. 5) to end, ending last rep. k. 3.
Row 2: P. 1, (p. 2 tog. t.b.l., y.r.n., p. 1, y.r.n., p. 2 tog., p. 2) to end, ending last rep. p. 1.
Row 3: (K. 2 tog., y.fd., k. 3, y.fd., k. 2 tog. t.b.l.) to end.
Row 4: P.

Row 5: K. 6, (k. 2 tog., y.fd., k. 5) to last st., k. 1.
Row 6: P. 4, (p. 2 tog. t.b.l., y.r.n., p. 1, y.r.n., p. 2 tog., p. 2) to last 3 sts., p. 3.
Row 7: K. 4, (k. 2 tog., y.fd., k. 3, y.fd., k. 2 tog. t.b.l.) to last 3 sts., k. 3.
Row 8: P.
These 8 rows form patt. Patt. until work measures 62 cm. Cast off.

Left front
With 2¾ mm. needles, cast on 60 (66, 72) sts. Work as Back to **.
Inc. row: Rib 6 (7, 8), * inc. in next st., rib 4; rep. from * to last 4 sts., rib 4 – 70 (77, 84) sts.
Change to 4 mm. needles and patt. as Back until work measures 62 cm. from beg., ending with a wrong side row.
Next row: Cast off 42 (49, 56) sts., patt. to end. Patt. 12 cm. on these 28 sts. for collar. Cast off loosely.

Right front
As Left Front, until work measures 62 cm., ending with a right side row.
Next row: Cast off 42 (49, 56) sts., patt. to end. Patt. 12 cm. on these 28 sts. for collar. Cast off loosely.

Sleeves
With 2¾ mm. needles, cast on 48 sts. Rep. rows 1 and 2 as beg. of Back thirteen times, then row 1 again.
Inc. row: K. 3, inc. in every st. to last 2 sts., k. 2 – 91 sts.
Change to 4 mm. needles and patt. as Back until work measures 31 cm. Cast off.

Front borders
Join front shoulders to 18 (21, 24) cm. at each end of Back.
With 3¼ mm. needles and right side facing, pick up and k. 168 sts. up right

front edge to cast-off edge of collar. Beg. with a row 2, rib 5 rows as beg. of Back.
Next row (make buttonholes): Rib 6, cast off 3, (rib 12, cast off 3) six times, rib to end.
Next row: Rib to end, casting on 3 sts. over those cast off in previous row. Rib 4 rows. Cast off ribwise.
With right side facing, beg. at cast-off edge of left front collar, work other side to match, omitting buttonholes.

TO MAKE UP

Press work. Beg. and ending 19.5 cm. from shoulder seams, sew sleeves to sides. Join side and sleeve seams. Join cast-off edges of collar. Setting this seam to centre, sew collar to back neck, easing in fullness. (When collar is rolled to right side, reverse side of pattern will be right side). Sew on buttons.

Loose cardigan in fancy trellis stitch, with a small shawl collar.

Red Hot

Classic cotton sweater with raglan sleeves, which couldn't be easier to knit. It's knitted in garter stitch (knit every row), and has a plain round neck.
Very easy

MATERIALS

10 (11, 12) 50 g. balls Pingouin Coton Naturel 8 Fils; a pair each 4 mm. (no. 8) and 6 mm. (no. 4) knitting needles.

TENSION

15 stitches and 19 rows to 10 cm. over garter stitch, using 6 mm. needles.

MEASUREMENTS

To fit bust 34 (36, 38) in., 86 (91, 97) cm.
Length 23¼ (24¾, 25½) in., 59 (63, 65) cm.
Sleeve (all sizes) 17½ in., 44 cm.

ABBREVIATIONS

k., knit; p., purl; st(s)., stitch(es); alt., alternate; beg., beginning; cont., continue; dec., decrease; foll., following; g-st., garter stitch; inc., increase; rem., remaining; rep., repeat; tog., together.

INSTRUCTIONS

Back

With 4 mm. needles, cast on 72 (76, 80) sts. Work in k. 1, p. 1 rib for 17 rows. Change to 6 mm. needles and work in g-st. (see page 13) until work measures 42 (44, 44) cm.

To shape raglan Row 1: K. 3, k. 2 tog., k. to last 5 sts., k. 2 tog., k. 3.
Row 2: K. 1, p. 2, k. to last 3 sts., p. 2, k. 1 **.

Rep. these 2 rows until 40 sts. remain, ending with a row 2. Cast off.

Front

Work as for Back to **. Rep. these 2 rows until 46 sts. remain, ending with a row 2.

To shape neck K. 3, k. 2 tog., k. 6, turn, leaving rem. sts. on spare needle.
Next row: K. 2 tog., k. to last 3 sts., p. 2, k. 1.
Cont. to shape raglan as set, but dec. 1 st. at neck edge on every alt. row until 3 sts. remain.
Next row: K. 1, k. 2 tog.
Next row: K. 2 tog. and fasten off.
Rejoin yarn to rem. sts. at neck edge, cast off centre 24 sts. for neck, k. to last 5 sts., k. 2 tog., k. 3. Complete to match first side, reversing shapings.

Sleeves

With 4 mm. needles, cast on 38 (42, 46) sts. Work in k. 1, p. 1 rib for 17 rows. Change to 6 mm. needles and work in g-st., at the same time inc. 1 st. at each end of ninth and every foll. tenth row until there are 52 (56, 60) sts. When work measures 44 cm., shape raglan.

To shape raglan Row 1: K. 3, k. 2 tog., k. to last 5 sts., k. 2 tog., k. 3.
Row 2: K. 1, p. 2, k. to last 3 sts., p. 2, k. 1.
Rep. these 2 rows until 20 sts. remain. Cast off.

TO MAKE UP

Join raglan seams except left back seam. Join side seams and sleeve seams.

Neckband

With right side facing and using 4 mm. needles, beg. at left back edge, pick up and k. 20 sts. over left sleeve top, 6 sts. along left side neck, 22 sts. along centre neck, 6 sts. along right side neck, 20 sts. along right sleeve top and 38 sts. along back neck edge – 112 sts.
Work 7 rows in k. 1, p. 1 rib, then cast off ribwise. Join neckband and left raglan seam.

Daisy

MATERIALS

10 (11, 11) 100 g. balls Twilleys Pegasus 100% cotton in main shade (white) or 9 (10, 10) balls if knitting the garment to the shorter length; 1 100 g. ball Twilleys Pegasus 100% cotton in contrast shade (peacock blue); a pair each 3¼ mm. (no. 10) and 3¾ mm. (no. 9) knitting needles; a cable needle.

TENSION

21 stitches and 28 rows to 10 cm. over stocking stitch.

MEASUREMENTS

To fit bust 34 (36, 38) in., 86 (91, 97) cm.
Length 31 (31½, 32) in., 79 (80, 81) cm. or, if preferred, the shorter classic length of 24 (24¼, 24¾) in., 61 (62, 63) cm.
Sleeve (all sizes) 17 in., 43 cm.

ABBREVIATIONS

k., knit; p., purl; st(s)., stitch(es); alt., alternate; beg., beginning; cont., continue; C5F, slip next 5 sts. onto cable needle and hold at front of work, k. 5 from left hand needle, then k. 5 from cable needle; dec(s)., decrease(s); foll., following; inc(s)., increase(s); patt., pattern; rep., repeat; sep., separately; st. st., stocking stitch; MS, main shade (white); CS, contrast shade (peacock blue).

INSTRUCTIONS

Back

With 3¼ mm. needles and MS, cast on 104 (108, 112) sts. Work in k. 1, p. 1 rib for 7 rows. Change to CS and work in k. 1, p. 1 rib for 2 rows. Change to MS and work in k. 1, p. 1 rib for 2 rows. Change to CS and work in k. 1, p. 1 for 2 rows. Change to MS and work in k. 1, p. 1 rib for 6 rows *.
Change to 3¾ mm. needles and work cable as follows:
Row 1: K. 47 (49, 51), p. 2, k. 1, inc. 1 st. into next 4 sts., k. 1, p. 2, k. 47 (49, 51) – 108 (112, 116) sts.
Cont. to work cable as below but when working row 1 thereafter do not work any incs. (i.e. row 1: k. 47 (49, 51), p. 2, k. 10, p. 2, k. 47 (49, 51).
Row 2: P. 47 (49, 51), k. 2, p. 10, k. 2, p. 47 (49, 51).
Rep. rows 1 and 2 twice more.
Row 7: K. 47 (49, 51), p. 2, C5F, p. 2, k. 47 (49, 51).
Row 8: As row 2.
Work rows 1 and 2 four times more. These 16 rows form patt. When patt. has been worked ten times in all (if working shorter length, work patt. seven times in all), shape armholes **.

To shape armholes Cast off 6 sts. at beg. of next 2 rows, and 3 sts. at beg. of foll. 2 rows, then dec. 1 st. at each end of next 3 alt. rows – 84 (88, 92) sts.
Cont. straight in patt. until work measures 17 (18, 19) cm. from beg. of armhole shaping. On a wrong side row, dec. 4 sts. over the cable while working normal patt. row – 80 (84, 88) sts.

To shape neck K. 26 (28, 30), cast off middle 28 sts., k. 26 (28, 30). Finish each side sep. Dec. 1 st. at neck edge on every row until 22 (24, 26) sts. remain. Cast off. Rejoin yarn and complete other side of neck to match, reversing shaping.

Front

Exactly as Back to **, working 4 decs. over cable on last wrong side row.

To shape armholes and neck Cast off 6 sts., work 45 (47, 49) sts., place centre 2 sts. on a safety-pin to be worked later as neckband. Finish each side sep. Cont. to shape armholes exactly as Back, but at neck edge dec. 1 st. on next and every foll. third row until 22 (24, 26) sts. remain. When work from beg. of armhole shaping measures the same as that of Back, cast off. Rejoin yarn and complete other side of neck to match, reversing shapings.

Sleeves

With 3¼ mm. needles and MS, cast on 48 (52, 56) sts. Work rib exactly as for Back to *, working 12 incs. evenly along last rib row – 60 (64, 68) sts.
Change to 3¾ mm. needles and work in st. st. (see page 13), but inc. 1 st. at each end of every foll. twelfth row until there are 70 (74, 78) sts. When work measures 43 cm. from beg., shape top.

To shape top
Cast off 5 sts. at beg. of next 2 rows, and 3 sts. at beg. of foll. 2 rows, then dec. 1 st. at each end of every alt. row until 28 sts. remain. Cast off 4 sts. at beg. of next 2 rows. Cast off remaining sts.

TO MAKE UP

Press all st. st. with a warm iron and a damp cloth on the reverse side. Join right shoulder seam.

Neckband

With 3¼ mm. needles and right side facing and with MS, beg. at left neck edge and pick up and k. 45 (47, 49) sts. along left neck edge, k. the 2 sts. from safety-pin, pick up and k. 45 (47, 49) sts. along right neck edge and 38 (40, 42) sts. along back neck. Work in k. 1, p. 1 rib for 4 rows, but dec. 1 st. at either side of the 2 central sts. on every alt. row throughout neckband. When fourth MS row has been completed, work 2 rows in CS, 2 rows in MS, 2 rows in CS to form 2 CS stripes. Now work 3 rows in MS, all the time working the front decs. Cast off ribwise. Join left shoulder seam and neckband. Set in sleeves. Join sleeve seams and side seams. Press all seams.

The French Lieutenant's Woman

MATERIALS

20 (21) 50 g. balls Lister Lee Thermo-Knit Chunky; a pair 6½ mm. (no. 3) knitting needles; eight large and four small gilt buttons; two 3 cm. gilt buckles; a 4.00 mm. crochet hook.

TENSION

10 stitches and 24 rows to 9 cm.

MEASUREMENTS

To fit bust 34-36 (38-40) in., 86-91 (97-102) cm. loosely.
Length (both sizes) 26¾ in., 68 cm.
Sleeve (both sizes) 15¾ in., 40 cm.

ABBREVIATIONS

k., knit; p., purl; st(s)., stitch(es); beg., beginning; cont., continue; dec., decrease; inc., increase; k. 1b., knit one below; patt., pattern; rep., repeat; st. st., stocking stitch; tog., together.

INSTRUCTIONS

Back
Cast on 63 (67) sts. K. 1 row. Patt. thus:
Row 1 (right side): K. 1, (k. next st. 1 row below st. on needle, slipping st. above off needle in the usual way – referred to as k. 1b., k. 1) to end.
Row 2: K. 2, (k. 1b., k. 1) to last st., k. 1. These 2 rows form rib patt. *. Patt. straight until work measures 68 cm. Cast off loosely.

Fronts (*both alike*)
Cast on 29 (31) sts. Work as Back to *. Patt. until work measures 20 cm. **.
Pocket opening row: Patt. 9 (10), cast off 11, patt. 9 (10).
Next row: Patt. 9 (10), turn; cast on 11 sts., turn; patt. 9 (10) **. Patt. straight until work measures 48 cm. Rep. from ** to ** once more. Patt. straight until work measures 68 cm. Cast off loosely.

Sleeves
Cast on 43 (47) sts. Work as Back to *. Patt. straight until work measures 40 cm. Cast off very loosely.

Neckband
Join 17 (19) sts. at each end of cast-off edge of Back to corresponding sts. of Fronts for shoulder seams. With right side facing, pick up and k. 12 sts. across right front neck, 29 sts. around back neck and 12 sts. across left front neck. Work 9 rows in k. 1, p. 1 rib, beg. second row p. 1. Cast off ribwise.

Front bands
Cast on 9 sts.
Row 1: K. 2, (p. 1, k. 1) to last st., k. 1.
Row 2: K. 1, (p. 1, k. 1) to end *.
Rep. rows 1 and 2 until work measures 5 cm.
Next row (buttonhole row): Rib 3, cast off 3, rib 3.
Next row: Rib 3, cast on 3, rib 3. Cont. in rib as set, making 7 more buttonholes, spaced 8.5 cm. apart (measure from base of previous buttonhole). Rib a further 3 cm. Cast off ribwise. Work another band to match, omitting buttonholes.

Epaulettes (*two*)
Work as Front Bands to *. Rep. 2 rib rows until band measures 19 (21) cm. Cast off ribwise.

Sleeve straps (*two*)
Cast on 5 sts. Rib 40 (44) cm. as Front Bands. Cast off ribwise.

Pocket linings (*four*)
Cast on 15 sts. Beg. k., work in st. st. (see page 13) until work measures 20 cm. Cast off.

TO MAKE UP

Do not press. Beg. and ending 19.5 (21.5) cm. from shoulder seams, sew cast-off edge of sleeves on sides of main part. Join side and sleeve seams. Sew cast-on edge of epaulettes along sleeve seams, matching centre to shoulder seams, then sew cast-off edges along base of neckband. Sew buckle on one end of each sleeve strap and sew this end to sleeves, 10 cm. from edge and 14 cm. from seams towards front of sleeves. Fasten straps around sleeves. Sew on front bands and 8 large buttons. Sew on pocket linings thus: with right side of lining facing, sew cast-on edge on wrong side of front just below cast-off edge of pocket. Fold up lining and sew cast-off edge just above cast-on edge of pocket; join side seams. Crochet 4 lengths of chain each 5 cm. long for button loops. Fold in half and sew ends tog. on centre top edge of each pocket. Sew small buttons on lower edges to correspond.

Foxfire

MATERIALS

Sweater 18 (19) 50 g. balls Sirdar Pullman (terra cotta – shade 104); a pair each 5½ mm. (no. 5) and 6½ mm. (no. 3) knitting needles; a cable needle.
Scarf-hat 4 50 g. balls Sirdar Pullman (terra cotta – shade 104); a pair 6½ mm. (no. 3) knitting needles; a cable needle; a 6.00 mm. crochet hook.

TENSION

15 stitches (one pattern) to 7.5 cm.; 14 rows (one pattern) to 8 cm.; 14 stitches to 10 cm. over stocking stitch.

MEASUREMENTS

Sweater: to fit bust 34 (36) in., 86 (91) cm.
Length (both sizes) 23½ in., 60 cm.
Sleeve with turned-back cuff (both sizes) 17½ in., 44 cm.

ABBREVIATIONS

k., knit; p., purl; st(s)., stitch(es); alt., alternate; beg., beginning; CF10, cable forward over 10 sts.; ch., chain; cont., continue; d.c., double crochet; dec., decrease; inc(s)., increase(s); patt., pattern; rep., repeat; sl., slip; s.s., slip stitch; st. st., stocking stitch.

INSTRUCTIONS

Sweater

Back and front (*both alike*)
With 5½ mm. needles, cast on 78 (82) sts. Work 8 rows in k. 2, p. 2 rib, beg. second row p. 2, and working 4 incs. evenly along last rib row – 82 (86) sts.
Change to 6½ mm. needles and patt. thus:
Row 1: P. 6, k. 10, * p. 5 (6), k. 10; rep. from * to last 6 sts., p. 6.
Row 2: K. 6, p. 10, * k. 5 (6), p. 10; rep. from * to last 6 sts., k. 6.

Boldly cabled sweater with a slashed neck has a matching scarf-hat with a cable.
Easy

Rep. rows 1 and 2 twice more.
Row 7: P. 6, sl. next 5 sts. onto a cable needle and hold at front of work, k. next 5 sts. from left hand needle, then k. 5 sts. from cable needle (called CF10), * p. 5 (6).
Row 8: As row 2.
Rows 9 to 14: Rep. rows 1 and 2 three times.
These 14 rows form patt.
Patt. until tenth row of seventh patt. has been completed. Change to 5½ mm. needles and rib 8 rows as beg. Cast off loosely.

Sleeves

With 5½ mm. needles, cast on 50 (50) sts. Rib 18 rows as Back and Front, but inc. 1 st. at each end of last of these rows for both sizes – 52 (54) sts.
Change to 6½ mm. needles and patt. as Back until sixth patt. is completed. Cast off.

Scarf-hat

With 6½ mm. needles cast on 96 sts. P. one row, k. one row. Beg. p. (right side), cont. in reversed st. st. (see page 13) and dec. 1 st. at each end of next and every alt. row until 2 sts. remain. Cast off.

Brim

With 6½ mm. needles, cast on 22 sts.
Row 1: P. 6, k. 10, p. 6.
Row 2: K. 6, p. 10, k. 6.
Rep. rows 1 and 2 twice more.
Row 7: P. 6, CF10, p. 6.
Row 8: As row 2.
Rep. rows 1 and 2 three times more. These 14 rows form patt. Patt. until eighth patt. has been completed. Cast off.

TO MAKE UP

Press work very lightly according to instructions on ball band.
Sweater: Join 26 (28) sts. at each end of cast-off edges of Back and Front for shoulders. Beg. and ending 14.5 (15) cm. from shoulder seams, sew cast-off edge of sleeves to sides of main part. Join side and sleeve seams, reversing seam for 6 cm. turn-back cuff.

Scarf-hat: With right side of scarf facing, rejoin yarn at one corner, and crochet 1 row d.c. around all 3 edges, s.s. to 1 ch. Fasten off. Along cast-on edge of scarf, fold hem of 4 cm. to wrong side and, omitting 10 cm. at each end, catch stitch. With right side of cable brim to wrong side of scarf, sew one long edge along hemline, still omitting 10 cm. at each end. Turn brim back flat onto right side of scarf and, omitting 7 cm. at each end, catch stitch other edge. Allow turn-back to roll over from stitching line of hem. Omitting 6 sts. towards hem, join cast-on and cast-off edges of cable brim.
Knot ends at back.

Claudine

See model (front), facing page

MATERIALS

6 (7, 8) 100 g. balls Twilleys Pegasus,
Twilleys Handicraft Cotton No. 1, *or*
Twilleys Handicraft Cotton D. 42; a pair
each 3¼ mm. (no. 10) and 3¾ mm. (no.
9) knitting needles; a cable needle; a
stitch-holder.

TENSION

10 stitches and 14 rows to 5 cm. over
pattern.

MEASUREMENTS

To fit bust 34 (36, 38) in., 86 (91, 97)
cm.
Length 23 (24, 24½) in., 60 (61, 62) cm.

ABBREVIATIONS

k., knit; p., purl; st(s)., stitch(es); alt.,
alternate; beg., beginning; B1, (k. 1, p. 1,
k. 1, p. 1) all into next st., turn and p. 4,
turn and k. 4, lift the 2nd, 3rd and 4th sts.
over the 1st, forming bobble; cont., continue; Cr2L, slip next 2 sts. onto cable
needle and hold at front of work, p. 1
from left hand needle, then k. 2 from
cable needle; Cr2R, slip next st. onto
cable needle and hold at back of work, k.
2 from left hand needle, then p. 1 from
cable needle; dec., decrease(e)(ing); inc.,
increase; patt., pattern; rep., repeat.

INSTRUCTIONS

Back
With 3¼ mm. needles, cast on 94 (100,
106) sts. Work 5 cm. in k. 1, p. 1 rib.
Change to 3¾ mm. needles and cont. in
patt. thus:
Row 1: P. 5 (8, 11), * p. 3, k. 2, p. 9 *,
rep. from * to * to last 5 (8, 11) sts., p. 5
(8, 11).
Row 2 and alt. rows: K. the k. sts. and p.
the p. sts.
Row 3: P. 5 (8, 11), * p. 3, Cr2L, p. 8 *,
rep. from * to * to last 5 (8, 11) sts., p. 5
(8, 11).
Row 5: P. 5 (8, 11), * p. 4, Cr2L, p. 7 *,
rep. from * to * to last 5 (8, 11) sts., p. 5
(8, 11).
Row 7: P. 5 (8, 11), * p. 5, Cr2L, p. 6 *,
rep. from * to * to last 5 (8, 11) sts., p. 5
(8, 11).
Row 9: P. 5 (8, 11), * p. 6, Cr2L, p. 5 *,
rep. from * to * to last 5 (8, 11) sts., p. 5
(8, 11).
Row 11: P. 5 (8, 11), * p. 7, Cr2L, p. 4 *,
rep. from * to * to last 5 (8, 11) sts., p. 5
(8, 11).
Row 13: P. 5 (8, 11), * p. 5, B1 into next
st., p. 2, Cr2L, p. 3 *, rep. from * to * to
last 5 (8, 11) sts., p. 5 (8, 11).
Row 15: P. 5 (8, 11), * p. 8, Cr2R, p. 3 *,
rep. from * to * to last 5 (8, 11) sts., p. 5
(8, 11).
Row 17: P. 5 (8, 11), * p. 7, Cr2R, p. 4 *,
rep. from * to * to last 5 (8, 11) sts., p. 5
(8, 11).
Row 19: P. 5 (8, 11), * p. 6, Cr2R, p. 5 *,
rep. from * to * to last 5 (8, 11) sts., p. 5
(8, 11).
Row 21: P. 5 (8, 11), * p. 5, Cr2R, p. 6 *,
rep. from * to * to last 5 (8, 11) sts., p. 5
(8, 11).
Row 23: P. 5 (8, 11), * p. 4, Cr2R, p. 7 *,
rep. from * to * to last 5 (8, 11) sts., p. 5
(8, 11).
Row 25: P. 5 (8, 11), * p. 3, Cr2R, p. 2,
B1 into next st., p. 5 *, rep. from * to * to
last 5 (8, 11) sts., p. 5 (8, 11).
Row 27: P. 5 (8, 11), * p. 3, Cr2L, p. 8 *,
rep. from * to * to last 5 (8, 11) sts., p. 5
(8, 11).
Row 28: As row 2.
When rows 1 to 28 have been completed once, work rows 5 to 28 only
thereafter, as these 24 rows form patt.
Cont. in patt. until work measures 40
cm. from beg.

Claudine

To shape armholes Cast off 4 sts. at beg. of next 2 rows, then dec. 1 st. at each end of next 3 alt. rows – 80 (86, 92) sts. **. Cont. straight until work measures 18 (19, 20) cm. from beg. of armhole shaping.

To shape neck Patt. 28 (30, 32) sts., place centre 24 (26, 28) sts. on a stitch-holder, patt. to end. Cont. on these sts., dec. 1 st. at neck edge on every row until 20 (22, 24) sts. remain. Cast off. Rejoin yarn and complete other side of neck to match.

Front
As Back to **. Cont. straight until work measures 14 (15, 16) cm. from beg. of armhole shaping.

To shape neck Patt. 30 (32, 34) sts., place centre 20 (22, 24) sts. on a stitch-holder, patt. to end. Cont. on these sts., dec. 1 st. at neck edge on every row until 20 (22, 24) sts. remain. Cont. straight until work measures same as Back to shoulder, then cast off. Complete other side of neck to match.

Neckband
Join right shoulder seam. With right side facing and 3¼ mm. needles, pick up and k. 16 sts. along left neck edge, k. across 20 (22, 24) sts. of centre front neck, pick up and k. 16 sts. along right neck edge, 10 sts. along right back neck, k. across 24 (26, 28) sts. of centre back neck and pick up and k. 10 sts. along left back neck edge – 96 (100, 104) sts. Work 5 rows in k. 1, p. 1 rib. Cast off ribwise.

Armbands
Join left shoulder and neckband seam. With right side facing and 3¼ mm. needles, pick up and k. 92 (96, 100) sts. evenly along armhole edge. Work 5 rows in k. 1, p. 1 rib. Cast off ribwise.

TO MAKE UP

Join side seams and armbands. Press seams lightly.

Annie

Cotton jacket in moss stitch with bobble and fern patterns on each front. The band is moss stitch and wooden buttons look good with the cotton.

See model (back), previous page

MATERIALS

9 (10, 10) 100 g. balls Twilleys Pegasus, Twilleys Handicraft Cotton No. 1, *or* Twilleys Handicraft Cotton D. 42; a pair each 3¾ mm. (no. 10) and 4 mm. (no. 8) knitting needles; a cable needle; five buttons.

TENSION

17 stitches and 28 rows to 10 cm. over moss stitch; 10 stitches and 14 rows to 5 cm. over reverse stocking stitch.

MEASUREMENTS

To fit bust 34 (36, 38) in., 86 (91, 97) cm.
Length 23½ (24, 24½) in., 60 (61, 62) cm.
Sleeve (all sizes) 17 in., 43 cm.

ABBREVIATIONS

k., knit; p., purl; st(s)., stitch(es); alt., alternate; BC, slip next st. onto cable needle and hold at back of work, k. the next st. on left hand needle, then p. the st. from cable needle; beg., beginning; BKC, slip next st. onto cable needle and hold at back of work, k. the next st. from left hand needle, then k. the st. from the cable needle; cont., continue; dec., decrease; FC, as BC, but hold the st. on cable needle at front of work; FKC, as BKC, but hold the st. on the cable needle at front of work; foll., following; inc(s)., increase(s); make bobble, (k. 1, p. 1, k. 1, p. 1) all into next st., turn and p. 4, turn and k. 4, p. 2 tog. twice, then k. 2 tog.; m. st., moss stitch; patt., pattern; rem., remaining; st. st., stocking stitch; tog., together.

INSTRUCTIONS

Back
With 3¾ mm. needles, cast on 80 (84, 88) sts.
Row 1: K. 1, p. 1 to end.
Row 2: P. 1, k. 1 to end.
These 2 rows form m. st. (see also page 13). Cont. in m. st. until work measures 40 cm. from beg.

To shape armholes Cast off 5 sts. at beg. of next 2 rows and 2 sts. at beg. of foll. 2 rows. Dec. 1 st. at each end of next 3 alt. rows – 60 (64, 68) sts.
Cont. until work measures 20 (21, 22) cm. from beg. of armhole shaping. Cast off.

Left front
With 3¾ mm. needles, cast on 50 (52, 54) sts. and work 11 rows in m. st.
Next row: Slip the 9 sts. of inside edge onto a safety-pin to be worked later as front band. Work one row more in m. st., working 7 incs. evenly along row – 48 (50, 52) sts.
Change to 4 mm. needles and cont. in patt. thus:
Row 1 (wrong side): (K. 7, p. 2, k. 7) three times to last 0 (2, 4) sts., k. 0 (2, 4).
Row 2: P. 0 (2, 4), (p. 7, k. 2, p. 7) three times.
Work rows 1 and 2 once more, then work row 1 again.
Row 6: P. 0 (2, 4), (p. 6, BKC, FKC, p. 6) three times.
Row 7: (K. 5, FC, p. 2, BC, k. 5) three times to last 0 (2, 4) sts., k. 0 (2, 4).
Row 8: P. 0 (2, 4), (p. 4, BC, BKC, FKC, FC, p. 4) three times.
Row 9: (K. 3, FC, k. 1, p. 4, k. 1, BC, k. 3) three times to last 0 (2, 4) sts., k. 0 (2, 4).
Row 10: P. 0, (2, 4), (p. 2, BC, p. 1, BC, k. 2, FC, p. 1, FC, p. 2) three times.
Row 11: (K. 2, p. 1, k. 2, p. 1, k. 1, p. 2, k. 1, p. 1, k. 2, p. 1, k. 2) three times to last 0 (2, 4) sts., k. 0 (2, 4).
Row 12: P. 0 (2, 4), p. 5, k. 1, p. 1, k. 2, p. 1, k. 1, p. 7, make bobble, p. 1, BC, p. 1, k. 2, p. 1, FC, p. 1, make bobble, p. 7, k. 1, p. 1, k. 2, p. 1, k. 1, p. 5.
Row 13: K. 5, p. 1, k. 1, p. 2, k. 1, p. 1, k. 9, p. 1, k. 2, p. 2, k. 2, p. 1, k. 9, p. 1, k. 1,

To shape top Cast off 5 sts. at beg. of next 2 rows, 2 sts. at beg. of foll. 2 rows then dec. 1 st. at each end of next 2 rows. Work 12 rows straight. Dec. 1 st. at each end of every alt. row until 24 sts. remain. Cast off 3 sts. at beg. of next 4 rows then cast off rem. sts.

Buttonhole band
Return to sts. on Right Front safety-pin.

Buttonhole row Work 4 sts. in m. st., cast off 2 sts., work to end.
Next row: Work 3 sts. in m. st., cast on 2 sts., work to end.
Work 22 rows in m. st. then rep. 2 buttonhole rows. When 5 buttonholes have been completed work band in m. st. until length reaches up neck edge and to centre of back neck, slightly stretched. Cast off.
Work left front band, omitting buttonholes, until length reaches up neck edge and to centre of back neck, slightly stretched. Cast off.

TO MAKE UP

Join shoulder seams. Set in sleeves. Join side and sleeve seams. Sew on front bands. Sew on buttons. Press seams lightly.

---

p. 2, k. 1, p. 1, k. 5 to last 0 (2, 4) sts., k. 0 (2, 4).
Row 14: P. 0 (2, 4), p. 7, k. 2, p. 11, make bobble, p. 2, k. 2, p. 2, make bobble, p. 11, k. 2, p. 7.
When patt. has been worked six times in all, work the centre bobble patt. only, working the rest of row in reversed st. st. (see page 13). Cont. until work measures 40 cm. from beg.

To shape armhole and neck Cast off 5 sts. at armhole edge, then 3 sts. on foll. alt. row. Dec. 1 st. at same edge on next 4 alt. rows, and at the same time dec. 1 st. at neck edge on next and every foll. fourth row until 20 sts. remain.
When centre patt. has been worked ten times from beg. work a bobble at top of last patt. completing a half circle of 5 bobbles and cont. in reverse st. st. only until work measures 20 (21, 22) cm. from beg. of armhole shaping. Cast off.

Right front
As Left Front, reversing all shaping.

Sleeves
With 3¾ mm. needles, cast on 44 (48, 52) sts. and k. 8 rows.
Inc. row: Inc. in every eighth st. — 49 (54, 58) sts.
Change to 4 mm. needles and work 20 cm. in m. st. Inc. 1 st. at each end of next and every foll. eighth row until there are 63 (68, 72) sts. Cont. until work measures 43 cm. from beg.

High Society

MATERIALS

13 (15) 25 g. balls Jaeger Mohair-Spun with Glitter; a pair each 5½ mm. (no. 5) and 6 mm. (no. 4) knitting needles; 200 ES12 beads; gold thread and a beading needle for sewing on beads; two shoulder pads.

TENSION

14 stitches and 20 rows to 10 cm. square.

MEASUREMENTS

To fit bust 32 (34) in., 81 (86) cm.
Length 23¼ (23¾) in., 59 (60) cm.
Sleeve seam (both sizes) 16½ in., 42 cm.

ABBREVIATIONS

k., knit; p., purl; st(s)., stitch(es); alt., alternate; beg., beginning; cont., continue; dec., decreas(e)(ing); foll., following; inc., increas(e)(ing); rem., remaining; st. st., stocking stitch; tog., together.

INSTRUCTIONS

Back
With 6 mm. needles, cast on 64 (68) sts. Beg. p. row, work in reversed st. st. (see page 13) until work measures 38 cm., ending with a k. row.

To shape raglan Cast off 2 sts. at beg. of next 2 rows. Work 2 rows straight. Dec. 1 st. at both ends of next row and every foll. fourth row until 46 (50) sts. remain, ending after a dec. row.

To shape neck Next row: K. 12 (14), cast off 22, k. to end. Cont. on last set of sts. thus:
Next row: P. to last 2 sts., p. 2 tog.
Next row: K.
Next row: P. 2 tog., p. to last 2 sts., p. 2 tog. – 9 (11) sts.
Work 2 (4) rows straight. Cast off. With

> **Simple mohair jacket with curved edges in reverse stocking stitch has beads scattered over the shoulders.**
> **Very easy**

right side facing, join yarn to rem. sts. and work to match first side, reversing shapings.

Left front
With 6 mm. needles, cast on 23 (24) sts. P. 1 row. Cont. in reverse st. st. as Back, inc. 1 st. at beg. of next row and foll. alt. rows until there are 30 (32) sts. Cont. straight until work is 10 rows less than Back to armhole, ending with a k. row.

To shape front Dec. 1 st. at end of next row and every foll. fourth row until 27 (29) sts. remain. Work 1 row, thus ending armhole edge.

To shape raglan Still dec. at front edge on every foll. fourth row from previous dec., cast off 2 sts. at beg. of next row, then dec. 1 st. at armhole edge on every foll. fourth row until 9 (11) sts. remain. Work 2 (4) rows straight. Cast off.

Right front
Work to match Left Front, reversing shapings, noting that inc. will be worked at end of second row instead of beg.

Sleeves
With 5½ mm. needles, cast on 30 (32) sts. Work 5 cm. in k. 1, p. 1 rib, inc. 6 (8) sts. evenly on last row – 36 (40) sts. Change to 6 mm. needles. Cont. in reverse st. st., inc. 1 st. at both ends of nineteenth row foll. and every foll. tenth row until there are 46 (50) sts. Cont. straight until work measures 42 cm., ending with a k. row.

To shape raglan Cast off 2 sts. at beg. of next 2 rows. Dec. 1 st. at both ends of next row and foll. alt. rows until 20 (22) sts. remain, then on every row until 14 (16) sts. remain. Cast off.

TO MAKE UP

Do not press. Join shoulder, side and sleeve seams. Sew in sleeves.
Edging: With 5½ mm. needles, cast on 8 sts.
Work in k. 1, p. 1 rib until edging fits all round outer edge. Cast off ribwise. Beg. and ending at right side seam, sew on edging. With gold thread, sew beads to upper part of jacket and sleeves as desired. Sew in shoulder pads.

Carrot Top

Simple mohair sweater knitted in reverse stocking stitch, with elbow-length sleeves, drawstrings and a round collar.
Very easy

MATERIALS

9 (10) 40 g. balls Pingouin Mohair (shade 302); a pair 5½ mm. (no. 5) knitting needles; a crochet hook.

TENSION

8 stitches and 9 rows to 5 cm.

MEASUREMENTS

To fit bust 34 (36) in., 86 (91) cm.
Length 20½ (21) in., 52 (53) cm.
Sleeve (both sizes) 14¼ in., 36 cm.

ABBREVIATIONS

k., knit; p., purl; st(s)., stitch(es); alt., alternate; beg., beginning; cont., continue; dec., decrease; foll., following; g-st., garter stitch; inc., increase; st. st., stocking stitch; tog., together; y.o.n., yarn over needle.

INSTRUCTIONS

Back

Cast on 50 (54) sts. Work 8 rows in k. 2, p. 2 rib (beg. second row p. 2).

Eyelet row: K. 2, (p. 2 tog., y.o.n., k. 2) to end. Rib one more row.
Inc. row (right side): P. 1, inc. purlwise in next st., to end – 75 (81) sts.
Beg. k., cont. in reversed st. st. (see page 13) until work measures 35 cm., ending with a k. row.

To shape armhole Cast off 7 sts. at beg. of next 2 rows *. Cont. straight until work measures 49 (50) cm., ending with a k. row.

To shape neck Next row: P. 22 (25), cast off 17, p. 22 (25). Cont. on last sts. only. Dec. 1 st. at neck edge on next and foll. alt. row. Work 1 row. Cast off. Complete other side to match.

Front
As Back to *.

To shape neck Next row: P. 25 (28), cast off 11, p. 25 (28). Cont. on last sts. only. Dec. 1 st. at neck edge on every alt. row until 20 (23) sts. remain. Cont. straight until work measures 52 (53) cm., ending at armhole. Cast off. Complete other side to match.

Sleeves

Cast on 28 (30) sts. Work 12 rows in k. 2, p. 2 rib. beg. second row p. 2 for 2nd size.
Inc. row (right side): Inc. purlwise in every st. – 56 (60) sts.
Beg. k., cont. in reversed st. st. until work measures 40.5 cm. Cast off.

Collar

Beg. at neck edge, cast on 70 sts. and work 4 rows in g-st. (see page 13).
Inc. row: Inc. in every st. – 140 sts.
Work 20 rows in g-st. Cast off loosely.

TO MAKE UP

Press very lightly. Join shoulder seams. Sew in sleeves, setting 4.5 cm. of sides of sleeves to cast-off groups at underarms. Join side and sleeve seams. Beg. and ending at centre back, sew collar to neck. With double yarn, crochet a 130 cm. length of chain. Thread chain through eyelets at lower edge to tie at centre front.

Bel-Gazou

Long baggy cotton top with a deep V-neck at front and back, which is knitted in moss stitch and single rib.
Very easy

MATERIALS

7 (8) 100 g. balls Twilleys Pegasus 100% cotton (lime green); a pair each 3¼ mm. (no. 10) and 4 mm. (no. 8) knitting needles.

TENSION

11 stitches and 16 rows to 6 cm. over moss stitch.

MEASUREMENTS

To fit bust 32-34 (36-38) in., 81-86 (92-97) cm.
Length 27 (27½) in., 69 (70) cm.

ABBREVIATIONS

k., knit; p., purl; st(s)., stitch(es); alt., alternate; beg., beginning; cont., continue; dec(s)., decrease(s); foll., following; inc., increase; patt., pattern; sep., separately.

INSTRUCTIONS

Front and back (*both alike*)
With 3¼ mm. needles, cast on 89 (95) sts. Work in k. 1, p. 1 rib for 17 rows. Change to 4 mm. needles and work in moss st. (*see page 13*) as follows:
Row 1: K. 1, p. 1 to last st., k. 1.
Row 2: K. the p. sts. and p. the k. sts. as they face you. These 2 rows form patt.
Work straight in patt. until work measures 48 cm. from beg.

To shape neck Work 44 (47), place the next st. on a safety-pin to be worked later as centre st. of neckband; work to end. Finish each side sep.
Dec. 1 st. at neck edge on next and every foll. third row. When 2 decs. have been completed, cont. to shape neck as set, but with right side facing.

To shape armholes (left side) At armhole edge, cast off 6 sts. at beg. of next row and 3 sts. at beg. of foll. alt. row. Now dec. 1 st. at same edge on every alt. row five times in all.
Cont. to shape neck as set until 10 sts. remain. Cast off. Rejoin yarn and complete right side of neck to match left. Join right shoulder seam.

Neckband
Mark the centre sts. at front and back neck with a coloured thread. With 3¼ mm. needles and right side facing, pick up and k. 50 (52) sts. along left neck edge, k. the centre st., pick up and k. 50 (52) sts. along right neck edge, pick up and k. 50 (52) sts. along back right neck edge, k. the back centre st., and pick up and k. 50 (52) sts. along back left neck edge. Now work in k. 1, p. 1 rib for 1 row. Work in k. 1, p. 1 rib for 5 rows more, but dec. 1 st. at either side of the centre sts. at front and back on every row. When the sixth rib row has been completed, cast off ribwise.

Armbands
Join left shoulder seam and neckband. With 3¼ mm. needles and right side facing, pick up and k. 96 (100) sts. along left armhole and work in k. 1, p. 1 rib for 5 rows. Cast off ribwise. Work right armhole to match.

TO MAKE UP

Join armbands and side seams. Press all seams.

Bowled Over

MATERIALS

9(10, 10) 100 g. balls Twilleys Pegasus in main shade (pink) and 1 ball in contrast shade (grey); a pair each 3¼ mm. (no. 10) and 4 mm. (no. 8) knitting needles; a cable needle.

TENSION

20 stitches and 26 rows to 10 cm. over stocking stitch.

MEASUREMENTS

To fit bust 34 (36, 38) in., 86 (91, 97) cm.
Length 30 (30½, 30¾) in., 76 (77, 78) cm.
Sleeve (all sizes) 17 in., 43 cm.

ABBREVIATIONS

k., knit; p., purl; st(s)., stitch(es); alt., alternate; beg., beginning; C6B, cable 6 back – slip the next 3 sts. onto cable needle and hold at back of work, k. 3, then k. 3 from cable needle; C6F, cable 6 forward – slip next 3 sts. onto cable needle and hold at front of work, k.3, then k. 3 from cable needle; dec(s)., decrease(s); foll., following; inc(s)., increase(s); MB, knit into the front and back of the st. 5 times in all to make 5 sts., y.r.n., then pass the 5 sts. one at a time over the y.r.n. and off needle; patt., pattern; rep., repeat; sep., separately; y.r.n., yarn round needle; MS, main shade (pink); CS, contrast shade (grey).

INSTRUCTIONS

Back

With 3¼ mm. needles and MS, cast on 93 (97, 101) sts. Work 3 rows in k. 1, p. 1 rib *. Change to CS and rib 2 rows, change to MS and rib 2 rows *. Work from * to * twice more. Change to CS and rib 2 rows, change to MS and rib 3 rows.

Unconventional cricket sweater with lots of texture. Team with a long cotton skirt or wear it as a mini dress.
Easy

Inc. row: Work 7 incs. evenly along rib row – 100 (104, 108) sts.
Change to 4 mm. needles and work patt. thus:
Row 1: K. 17 (19, 21), p. 2, k. 9, (p. 2, k. 12) three times, p. 2, k. 9, p. 2, k. 17 (19, 21).
Row 2 and alt. rows: K. the k. sts. and p. the p. sts. as they face you.
Row 3: K. 17 (19, 21), p. 2, C6B, k. 3, (p. 2, k. 12) three times, p. 2, k. 3, C6F, p. 2, k. 17 (19, 21).
Row 5: K. 17 (19, 21), p. 2, k. 1, MB, k. 7, p. 2, k. 12, p. 2, C6B, C6F, p. 2, k. 12, p. 2, k. 7, MB, k. 1, p. 2, k. 17 (19, 21).
Row 7: As row 1.
Row 9: K. 17 (19, 21), p. 2, k. 3, C6F, (p. 2, k. 12) three times, p. 2, C6B, k. 3, p. 2, k. 17 (19, 21).
Row 11: K. 17 (19, 21), p. 2, k. 7, MB, k. 1, p. 2, k. 12, p. 2, C6F, C6B, p. 2, k. 12, p. 2, k. 1, MB, k. 7, p. 2, k. 17 (19, 21).
Row 12: As row 2.
These 12 rows form patt. When patt. has been worked ten times in all, shape raglan **.

To shape raglan Cast off 2 sts. at beg. of next 2 rows – 96 (100, 104) sts.
Next row: K. 3, k. 2 tog., work in patt. to last 5 sts., k. 2 tog., k. 3.
Next row: P.
Rep. the last 2 rows until 38 sts. remain, working 6 decs. over centre cable on last row – 32 sts. Do not cast off.

Front

As Back to **.

To shape raglans and V-neck Cast off 2 sts. at beg. of next row, work in patt. over 47 (49, 51) sts., place next 2 sts. on a safety-pin to be worked later as neckband. Finish each side sep. Dec. 1 st. at

neck edge on next and every foll. third row. At the same time, work raglan at the outer edges as set for Back. Rejoin yarn and complete other side of neck to match.

Sleeves

With 3¼ mm. needles and MS, cast on 52 (56, 60) sts. Work rib with 4 CS stripes as set for Back. When the third rib row after the fourth stripe has been completed, work 18 incs. evenly along last rib row – 70 (74, 78) sts.
Change to 4 mm. needles and work the 12 row cable patt. as set for Back thus:
Row 1: K. 8 (10, 12), p. 2, k. 9, p. 2, k. 6, p. 2, k. 12, p. 2, k. 6, p. 2, k. 9, p. 2, k. 8 (10, 12).
Row 2 and alt. rows: K. the k. sts. and p. the p. sts. as they face you.
Row 3: K. 8 (10, 12), p. 2, C6B, k. 3, p. 2, k. 6, p. 2, k. 12, p. 2, k. 6, p. 2, k. 3, C6F, p. 2, k. 8 (10, 12).
Row 5: K. 8 (10, 12), p. 2, k. 1, MB, k. 7, p. 2, k. 6, p. 2, C6B, C6F, p. 2, k. 6, p. 2, k. 7, MB, k. 1, p. 2, k. 8 (10, 12).
Row 7: As row 1.
Row 9: K. 8 (10, 12), p. 2, k. 3, C6F, p. 2, k. 6, p. 2, k. 12, p. 2, k. 6, p. 2, C6B, k. 3, p. 2, k. 8 (10, 12).
Row 11: K. 8 (10, 12), p. 2, k. 7, MB, k. 1, p. 2, k. 6, p. 2, C6F, C6B, p. 2, k. 6, p. 2, k. 1, MB, k. 7, p. 2, k. 8 (10, 12).
Row 12: As row 2.
These 12 rows form patt. When patt. has been completed once, inc. 1 st. at each end of next and every foll. twelfth row. When patt. has been completed eight times in all, work last 2 incs. on the last eighth patt. row – 86 (90, 94) sts.

To shape raglan Dec. 1 st. at each end of next and every foll. alt. row until 28 sts. remain, working 6 decs. over centre cable on last row – 22 sts. Do not cast off.

Neckband

With 3¼ mm. needles and MS, work in k. 1, p. 1 rib over the 22 sts. of left sleeve, pick up and k. 46 sts. along left neck edge, k. the centre 2 sts., pick up and k. 46 sts. along right neck edge, work over the 22 sts. of right sleeve in k. 1, p. 1 rib, then work over the 32 sts. of back neck in

k. 1, p. 1 rib – 170 sts.
Now work the foll. rib rows, but dec. 1 st. at each side of the 2 centre neck sts. on every row. Work one more row in MS, then change to CS and rib 2 rows, change to MS and rib 2 rows, change to CS and rib 2 rows, and change to MS and rib 4 rows (making 2 stripes in CS). Cast off ribwise.

TO MAKE UP

Press stocking stitch parts of garment according to instructions on ball band. Join raglan seams and join neckband. Join side and sleeve seams.

Puffball

MATERIALS

16 25 g. balls Jaeger Mohair-Spun; a pair each 5 mm. (no. 6) and 6 mm. (no. 4) knitting needles.

TENSION

6 stitches to 5 cm.

MEASUREMENTS

To fit bust 34-38 in., 86-97 cm.
Length 26¼ in., 67 cm.

ABBREVIATIONS

k., knit; p., purl; st(s)., stitch(es); alt., alternate; beg., beginning; cont., continue; dec., decreas(e)(ing); foll., following; inc., increas(e)(ing); patt., pattern; p.s.s.o., pass slip stitch over; rem., remaining; rep., repeat; sl., slip; tog., together; y.f., yarn forward.

INSTRUCTIONS

The main part
Beg. at left cuff edge. With 5 mm. needles, cast on 35 sts. Work 12 rows in k. 1, p. 1 rib, beg. alt. rows p. 1.
Inc. row: (K. 1, p. 1, k. 1) in each st. to end – 105 sts.
Change to 6 mm. needles and patt. thus:
*Row 1 (*right side): P.
Row 2: K. 1, (y.f., k. 2 tog.) to end.
Row 3: P.
Row 4: (Sl. 1, k. 1, p.s.s.o., y.f.) to last st., k. 1.
Rep. rows 1 to 4 six times more, then rows 1 and 2 once more.

To shape sides Cast on 4 sts. at beg. of next 12 rows – 153 sts.
Patt. 34 rows straight.

To shape neck *Next row:* Patt. 75, turn and cont. on these sts. Dec. 1 st. at beg. of next row and at same edge on foll. 3 rows. Patt. 26 rows straight, thus ending

neck edge. Now inc. 1 st. at same edge on next 4 rows. Leave sts. for the time being.
With right side facing, join yarn to rem. sts. Cast off 3, patt. to end. Patt. 1 row straight. Cast off 2 sts. at beg. of next row and foll. 2 alt. rows, then dec. 1 st. at same edge on next 2 rows – 67 sts. Patt. 7 rows straight. Cast off. With 6 mm. needles, cast on 67 sts. Patt. 8 rows as Back.

To shape neck Inc. 1 st. at beg. of next row and at same edge on foll. row. Cast on 2 sts. at beg. of next row and foll. 2 alt. rows.
Next row: Patt. to end, turn and cast on 3 sts., turn and patt. across 75 sts. on spare needle – 153 sts.
Patt. 34 rows straight.

To shape sides Cast off 4 sts. at beg. of next 12 rows – 105 sts.
Patt. 28 rows straight. Change to 5 mm. needles.
Dec. row: (K. 3 tog.) to end – 35 sts.
Work 12 rows in k. 1, p. 1 rib as left cuff.
Cast off.

TO MAKE UP

Join side and sleeve seams.

The welt
With 5 mm. needles and right side facing, pick up and k. 152 sts. along lower edge. * Work 6 rows in k. 1, p. 1 rib, inc. 1 st. at both ends of every row. Cast off in rib *.

The front band
With 5 mm. needles and right side facing, pick up and k. 69 sts. up straight edge of right front, 58 sts. round neck, 69 sts. down straight edge of left front. Work as welt from * to *. Join shaped edges of welt and bands together.

Airy mohair summer jacket, knitted sideways on big needles in an easy lace stitch.
Easy

Tapestry

Only for the experts: a Fair Isle sweater with an overall pattern in blending shades on a pale pink background. Knitted all in one piece, the sweater has a big round neck and dolman sleeves.

MATERIALS

8 50 g. balls Pingouin Pingostar in main shade – light pink (no. 534), 1 ball in each of 4 contrast shades – light purple (no. 561), dark pink (no. 539), yellow (no. 562), and blue (no. 511), 2 balls in another contrast shade – grey (no. 505), and 3 balls in further contrast shade – dark purple (no. 557); a pair each 3¾ mm. (no. 9) and 4 mm. (no. 8) knitting needles; a circular 3¾ mm. (no. 9) knitting needle; a stitch-holder.

TENSION

30 stitches and 33 rows to 15 cm.

MEASUREMENTS

To fit bust 32-36 in., 82-91 cm.
Length 27½ in., 70 cm.
Sleeve 17½ in., 44 cm.

ABBREVIATIONS

k., knit; p., purl; st(s)., stitch(es); beg., beginning; cont., continue; dec(s)., decrease(s); foll., following; inc., increase; patt., pattern; rep., repeat.

INSTRUCTIONS

Beg. at front bottom edge. With 3¾ mm. needles and main shade, cast on 92 sts. Work in k. 1, p. 1 rib for 7 cm., ending with a wrong side row. Change to 4 mm. needles, and work Fair Isle from chart, working rows 1 to 60 once, then rows 1 to 12 once more.

To shape sleeves Cont. to work Fair Isle from chart, but inc. 1 st. at each end of every row for the next 14 rows – 120 sts.
Cast on 16 sts at beg. of next 2 rows, and 30 sts. at beg. of foll. 2 rows – 212 sts.
Cast on 15 sts. at beg. of next 2 rows – 242 sts.
Cont. second patt. rep. until row 58 of chart has been completed.

To shape front neck Work 110 sts. in patt., turn; work on these sts. only (left side of neck).
Cast off 4 sts., work to end. Dec. 1 st. at neck edge on every row fifteen times in all – 91 sts. Work straight until eighteenth row of third patt. rep. has been completed. Mark each end of row with a coloured thread and leave these sts. for the time being.
Slip the centre 22 sts. onto a stitch-holder to be worked later as neckband. Rejoin yarn and complete right side of neck to match left side.

To shape back neck Left side: Patt. 8 rows straight over 91 sts. Now cast on 2 sts. at neck edge on next 2 alt. rows – 95 sts.
Work right side to match.
Now cast on 52 sts. at neck edge at left side and join to right side – 242 sts.
Work straight in patt. until sixth row of fourth patt. rep. has been completed.

To shape sleeves (back) Cast off 15 sts. at beg. of next 2 rows, and 30 sts. at beg. of foll. 2 rows. Now cast off 16 sts. at beg. of next 2 rows. Dec. 1 st. at each end of every row for the next 14 rows – 92 sts.
Work straight until thirty-eighth row of fifth patt. rep. has been completed.
Change to 3¾ mm. needles and work in k. 1, p. 1 rib in main shade for 7 cm. Cast off.

Neckband

Beg. at right back neck edge. With 3¾ mm. circular needle, work in k. 1, p. 1 rib over the 52 sts. of back neck; pick up and k. 26 sts. along left neck edge, then, beg.

p. 1, work over the 22 sts. of front neck in k. 1, p. 1 rib; pick up and k. 26 sts. along right neck edge – 126 sts. Work in k. 1, p. 1 rib for 24 rows, then cast off ribwise.

Sleeve bands

With 3¾ mm. needles and right side facing and with main shade, pick up and k. 78 sts. along left sleeve edge.

Next row: K., but work 10 decs. evenly along row – 68 sts.

Work in k. 1, p. 1 rib for 7 cm., then cast off ribwise. Work band for right sleeve to match.

TO MAKE UP

Press very lightly with a warm iron and a damp cloth. Join side seams and sleeve bands. Fold neckband in half and stitch down on the inside. Press all seams.

KEY
Pingostar

● shade 505 (grey)
╱ shade 561 (light purple)
✕ shade 557 (dark purple)
▽ shade 539 (dark pink)
╲ shade 562 (yellow)
■ shade 511 (blue)
□ main shade 534 (light pink)

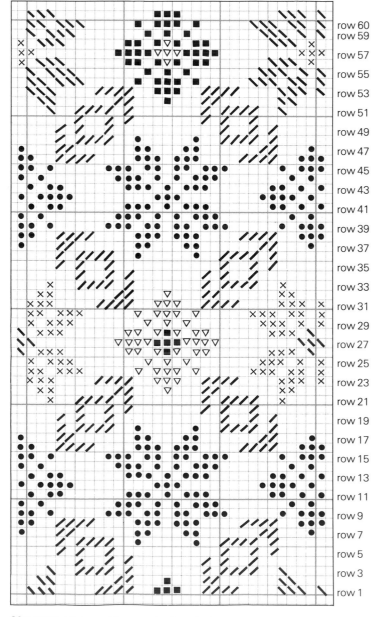

30 pattern stitches with one selvedge stitch at each end of every row